A Twentieth Century Fund Report

# THE CHALLENGE OF MEGALOPOLIS

A Graphic Presentation of the Urbanized
Northeastern Seaboard of the
United States

by Wolf Von Eckardt

Based on the original study by Jean Gottmann

The Macmillan Company/1964

# Contents

# Foreword

Megalopolis—meaning the huge string of central cities, suburbs and satellite areas that stretches along the eastern seaboard of the United States from north of Boston to south of Washington—is the largest, wealthiest and most productive urbanized region on earth.

It is a fascinating region to observe and to study on its own account. It becomes even more significant when we reflect upon the spread of industrial civilization and the very rapid growth of cities all over the globe. In this light we see that Megalopolis, in Jean Gottmann's expressive phrasing, "may be considered the cradle of a new order in the organization of inhabited space."

Megalopolis thus presents a major challenge to the whole of modern civilization. What is the structure and quality of life within Megalopolis? What kinds of activities go on there? What of its transportation, communications, food supply; its natural resources and productive capacity? What forces brought it into being and shaped its growth? How well is it equipped to deal with the problems that face it now and will face it in the evolving future?

It was to answer such questions as these that the Twentieth Century Fund undertook its original study of the region, resulting in the publication of an 810-page report, *Megalopolis: The Urbanized Northeastern Seaboard of the United States,* in 1961.

The author was Dr. Jean Gottmann, a Professor at the University of Paris and one of Europe's most distinguished geographers. His work at the Institute for Advanced Study, in Princeton, as well as an earlier study, *Virginia at Mid-Century,* had made him familiar with American ways of living and gave him sharp insights into our culture. He was the first to apply the term Megalopolis specifically to the northeastern seaboard of the United States.

The present book seeks to bring together some of his central findings, set forth in nontechnical language and reinforced by maps, drawings and graphic charts. The aim is to make the material available to the general reader, to school and college students, to public officials and civic planners, and to interested citizens not only in the United States but around the world.

It may be well to clear up one widespread misconception. When the orginal study of Megalopolis was first announced, most people immediately assumed that it would present an image of one monstrous city, a kind of indefinite extension of Times Square up and down the whole Atlantic seaboard. The reality, of course, is quite different. To many readers it comes as a surprise to learn that wooded areas and agricultural output are both actually *increasing* in Megalopolis.

This study is essentially hopeful in outlook. The reader will find here no cry of unrelieved urban doom and gloom—although the challenge to human ingenuity and energy is never underestimated.

The Fund was fortunate in persuading Wolf Von Eckardt, an architectural writer and critic who contributes to *Horizon, Harper's* and other periodicals and writes the weekly "Cityscape" column for the *Washington Post,* to undertake the preparation of the present book. Mr. Von Eckardt not only wrote the text, but planned and laid out all the graphics, designed the book, and did the page-by-page layouts. Stephen Kraft did the maps and drawings and the cover, following designs sketched by Von Eckardt. The author of the original study, Dr. Gottmann, carefully checked all the material in the present version.

Mrs. Louise Field, Research Associate, and Thomas R. Carskadon, Associate Director of the Fund, were helpful in editing and general supervision.

The Fund is grateful to Dr. Gottmann and Mr. Von Eckardt and to all the others who assisted in producing this book, which it hopes may contribute to a better understanding of the growth of large city-regions, a central phenomenon of our times.

August Heckscher,

*Director, The Twentieth Century Fund*

4

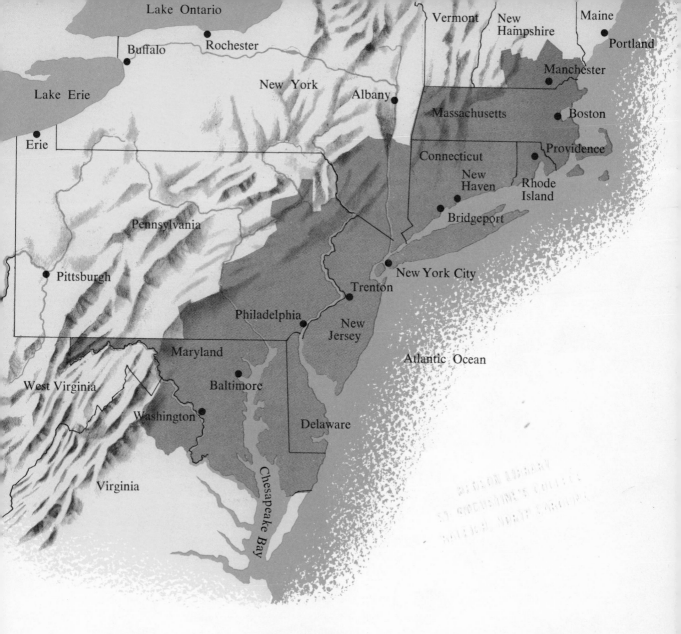

# 1 MEGALOPOLIS:

# A VERY SPECIAL REGION

Some two thousand years before the Pilgrims reached our shores, a group of ancient Greeks planned a new city-state in the Peloponnesus. They called it *Megalopolis,* or "very large city," because they dreamed that it would become the biggest and greatest of all the cities of Greece.

A few hundred years later the Jewish philosopher Philo of Alexandria applied the name Megalopolis to his concept of a city of ideas which would rule our material world.

Ancient Megalopolis still exists but it is only an insignificant town. It never became really large, let alone great. But the dream, it seems, has become true. In our country. Today.

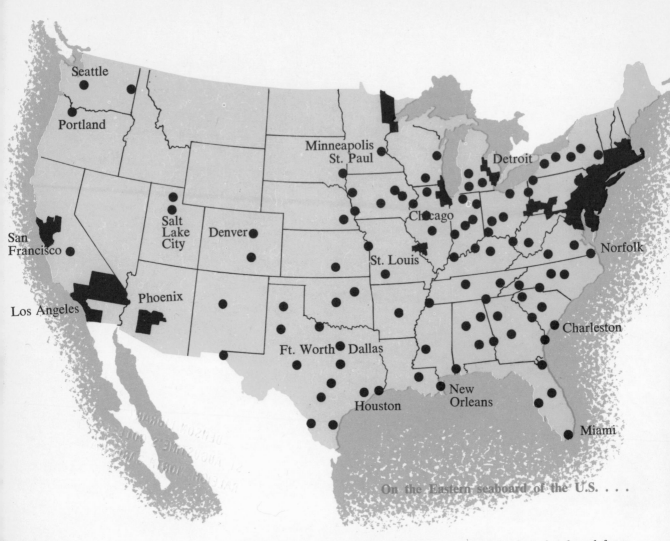

Seattle
Portland
Minneapolis
St. Paul
Detroit
Salt
Lake
City
Denver
San
Francisco
St. Louis
Chicago
Norfolk
Los Angeles
Phoenix
Charleston
Ft. Worth   Dallas
Houston
New
Orleans
Miami

On the Eastern seaboard of the U.S. . . .

One continuous stretch of cities and suburbs has developed from
southern New Hampshire to northern Virginia and from the Atlantic
shore to the Appalachian foothills.

No other region of the United States has such a large concentration
of people, living so close together, spread over such a large area of
land.

No other region has a comparable position in the nation or a comparable importance in the world. It has attained supremacy in politics,
in economics and probably also in culture.

It is a new type of region with a distinct personality of its own. Yet
it is also the result of age-old processes, such as the growth of cities,
the division of labor within civilized society, and the development of
world resources. Its personality evolved over three centuries.

It is difficult to identify this region precisely. Its limits cut across
established historical divisions such as New England or the Middle
Atlantic States.

Nor does it respect political boundaries. Some states are entirely
included, others only partly.

The region therefore needs a special name. As a place designation
that name should be new. As a symbol it should reflect the age-old

6

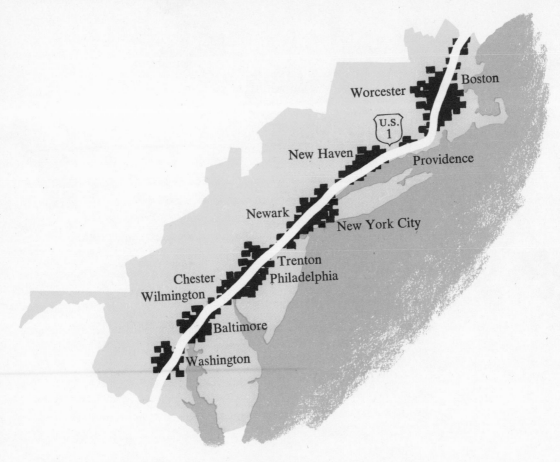

. . . the urban centers along the old highway U.S. 1 are growing together

human aspirations and endeavors that are at work here, that ancient Greek dream and ideal.

Hence the choice of the name Megalopolis.

**The distinction between city and country is gone.**

If you go by train from Boston to Washington, D. C., you see hardly anything but built-up areas, either tightly woven residential communities or concentrations of manufacturing plants.

If you drive or fly this route, however, you will discover large remaining areas of woods and brush alternating with patches of farmland. Yet, upon closer inspection, many of these seemingly rural areas turn out to be suburbs. They contain both residences and industry.

**Megalopolis is neither urban nor rural but suburban.**

The farms are seldom worked by people whose only occupation and source of income is agriculture. But neither can the life these people lead be properly called "urban."

In this area, then, our concept of the city as a tightly settled and organized unit, crowded with people, activities and riches, no longer

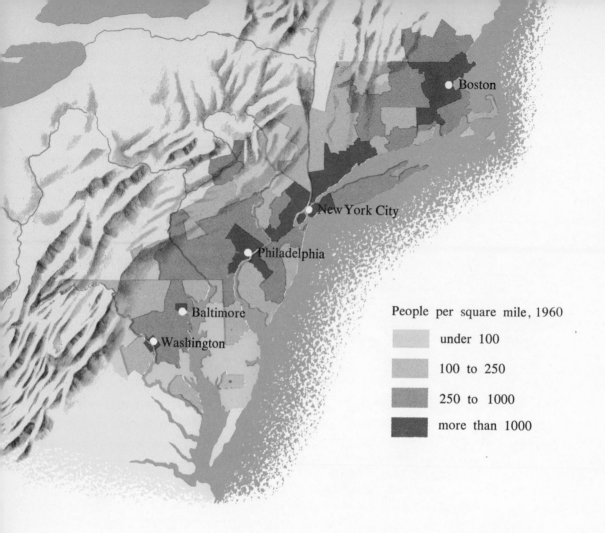

People per square mile, 1960

under 100

100 to 250

250 to 1000

more than 1000

Population density is greatest around the seaports

applies. Cities are no longer separated from their nonurban surroundings. They spread far and wide around their original center.

It is difficult to tell where one city ends and another begins. We have, rather, an almost continuous system of deeply interwoven urban and suburban areas.

**The most densely populated area in the country,**

Megalopolis is, however, far from being so overpopulated that there is poverty and want. On the contrary.

In 1960 the average population density of the area came close to 700 inhabitants per square mile. The national average was 51. Even the crowded western half of California approached only 210.

In the past we have generally considered such crowding bad.

We have mentally associated living close together with teeming tenements and all the evils of slums. In Megalopolis, as well as in the similarly populous areas of northwestern Europe, we find, however, that high population density is the result of urbanization and indus-

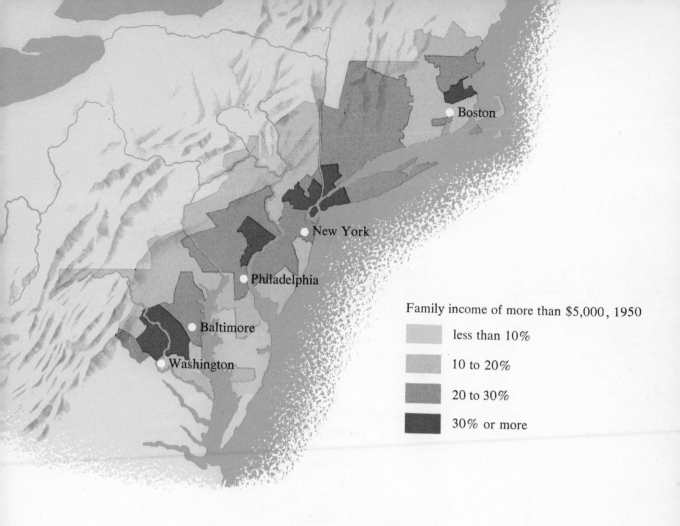

Family income of more than $5,000, 1950

- less than 10%
- 10 to 20%
- 20 to 30%
- 30% or more

High family income often coincides with high density

trialization. Here the old prejudice against population density is no longer justified. As the two maps show, high population density in Megalopolis coincides with high income and consequent affluence. Relative crowding has, in fact, contributed to wealth and power. It is a crowding of a rich *variety* of people engaged in a rich variety of activities.

Megalopolis is, of course, not the only place where this is happening.

Modern technology and social revolution give more and more people the opportunity to live and work in the city. At the same time more agricultural goods are produced with less manpower. These facts, coupled with the growth in population, swell cities everywhere. They are bursting their old limits and scattering all over the landscape.

But it happened first and most intensely in Megalopolis. That is why a study of the growth and challenge of this area provides both lessons and warnings. Megalopolis is the laboratory of a new urban way of life which is sweeping the civilized world.

# Earthly Bounds

Albany
Boston
Providence
Philadelphia
New York City
Baltimore
Washington
Richmond

**Inland navigation medium size vessels**

Summer   Winter

80
70
60
50
40
30
20
10
0

**Average temperature**

Lake Erie (to Midwest)

(to Mississippi valley)

Hudson
Delaware
Susquehanna
Potomac

**Westward routes**

Nature has put no obstacles in the way of the settlement and astounding development of Megalopolis. But neither is the region endowed with any extraordinary advantages.

There is, for instance, a remarkable variety of different kinds of soil. But little of it is of superior quality.

### There are scant mineral deposits.

The anthracite coalfields of northeastern Pennsylvania are important, of course. Such centers as Scranton, Wilkes-Barre and Reading developed because of their coal mines. But these riches would amount to little were they not easily accessible to the ports and population centers of Pennsylvania and New York.

The physical characteristic that accounts for the unique development of Megalopolis is primarily its location.

### Ideally located for shipping and trade.

Megalopolis stretches along the Atlantic Ocean, facing Europe. Flooded valleys form the great estuaries of the Hudson River, the Delaware Bay and the Chesapeake Bay. These allow seagoing and coastal vessels to go far inland, a boon to trade.

### The climate is moderate

because Megalopolis is located in the middle latitudes—between 43° and 38°. This means that the waterways seldom freeze. The weather favors agriculture, too. There is a growing season of more than 180 days that are free of killing frost. While heat and cold often seem extreme, the climate seldom interferes with commerce and industry.

### Easy access to inland regions

further helps Megalopolis' development. Topographically, the area divides into coastal lowlands along the Atlantic and the rugged foothills of the Appalachian ranges (which reach the coast in New England). Between the two is the Fall Line, so-called because it is marked by rapids and falls where the streams cross it. The mountain ranges are broken up and easier to cross than farther south. There are, in fact, several convenient corridors for both land and water transportation to the riches of the West.

### Proximity influenced economic development.

Being located so close together forced the towns of Megalopolis into competition and specialization. A division of labor developed, just as it did between people. This made the towns more dependent on one another. But competition helped all of them to grow despite the relatively small size of the area.

# Main Street of the Nation

For the nation as a whole Megalopolis is what Main Street is for most communities.

It is the place where government, most of the banks, the big offices, the newspapers and broadcasting stations, the important stores, the schools, libraries and theaters are concentrated.

It is the place where policies, decisions and fashions, or most of them, are made for the entire community. If Main Street is booming, the whole community prospers.

The same is true of Megalopolis in respect to the nation. It can be said, in fact, that the economic, political and cultural life of Megalopolis has become an essential factor in the economic, political and cultural life of the entire free world.

Foreign visitors rarely see more of America than Megalopolis, just as passing visitors in a town rarely see more than a few blocks of Main Street.

### The pre-eminence of Megalopolis is rooted in history.

The region is first in power and influence largely because it was here that the United States of America first began to emerge. The Pilgrims landed here. It was on the northeastern seaboard that the colonies declared their independence and the nation was born. And here, for three centuries, was the gateway for the transcontinental march of settlement.

As a result of that march ours is now a highly developed continent. It boasts at least two other concentrations of urban clusters, riches, economic equipment and educated people—the industrialized Midwest, between the Great Lakes and the Ohio River, and the California seaboard. But Megalopolis shows no signs of relinquishing its pre-eminent position to these. On the contrary, it continues to assume more of the Main Street functions than ever.

### The impact of the Federal government in Washington

on the everyday life of people throughout the country is not apt to lessen, regardless of politics. As the technological age becomes more complex, people are forced to specialize in their pursuits to earn their living. The more we specialize, the more need we have for central coordination of our common efforts in all our public activities.

When Washington was planned and built just below the falls of the Potomac, its planners expected it to develop into a great seaport and commercial center. Instead, it remained specialized as a city which serves the Federal government almost exclusively. And, as the nation grew, it also became an international center. This does not mean, however, that political and economic policy-making are, or ever have been, divorced. This would be impossible. Washington simply did not need to develop into an industrial and economic center because such centers are nearby and also within Megalopolis.

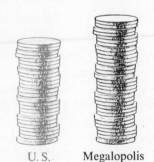

U. S. Population

Megalopolis

U. S.  Megalopolis

Average per capita income

Megalopolis

Large Libraries in U.S.

Number of mass
circulation magazines

Rest of     Megalopolis
U.S.

Large Advertising Agencies

Rest of     Megalopolis
U.S.

Bank Deposits

Rest of U.S.     Megalopolis

## The nation's money market

is, of course, predominantly located in New York. The largest financial institutions and the nation's two important security exchanges are in downtown Manhattan. And New York shares its tremendous concentration of financial power only with other Megalopolitan centers, mainly Boston, Philadelphia and, lately, Washington. Through the Securities and Exchange Commission and the Federal Reserve Board, Washington exercises the necessary controls over the money market. Since Federal expenditures and the trading in U.S. government securities are becoming increasingly important, Washington also plays a substantial part in the world of finance.

The insurance industry, too, which started in Megalopolis, is still mainly concentrated there.

## Finance and management have become inseparable

just as have political and economic policies. All managerial decision-making for industry and commerce, in fact, is deeply interwoven with financial problems. That is why most of the country's large corporations, no matter where their production centers may be, keep adding their imposing headquarters palaces to the skylines of Megalopolis.

## Mass communications

are almost exclusively concentrated in Megalopolis. One of the most important raw materials of the office industry is information. The countinghouses of old have grown into huge banks, stock exchanges and insurance companies. The exchange of news and gossip on the street and in taverns has been replaced by the great newspapers, the magazines, the broadcasting corporations and advertising.

And as we all know, Times Square and Madison Avenue wield the same influence on the nation's mass communications media as Wall Street and the midtown banks wield on the nation's financial affairs.

We need not elaborate on the influence of the big radio and television corporations on local stations and listeners across the country. Broadcasting is licensed in Washington, and the networks—CBS, NBC and ABC—are all headquartered in New York. Broadcasting stations, like newspapers, are local, of course. But the vast majority of them are affiliated with the big networks.

## Madison Avenue dominates advertising

and while not all big advertising agencies have their offices on that street, just about all the large and influential ones have their offices in Megalopolis. Again, this is quite logical, considering that both their clients (the industrial and commercial corporations) and their outlets (the mass communication media) are located there.

The complex modern integration of business and culture is demonstrated by the dependency of the mass communication media on advertising. Advertising accounts for 70 percent of the total revenue of newspapers, 60 percent of the revenue of magazines and 90 percent of the income of television stations.

**Life Insurance Companies**

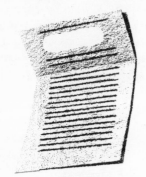

Rest of        Megalopolis
U.S.

**Stock Transactions**

Megalopolis

Rest of U.S.

**Newspaper Feature Services**

Rest of U.S.   Megalopolis

Public relations, a relatively new and pervasive aspect of our culture, is also more prevalent in Megalopolis than elsewhere.

### A thirst for education and culture

developed early in our history. As soon as our new society was settled sufficiently to do so, it established colleges, universities, symphony orchestras, theaters, and museums. Again the area between New Hampshire and Maryland had a head start in building reputation and nation-wide influence.

Such names as Harvard, Yale and Princeton, the New York Philharmonic, the Metropolitan Museum of Art, the Philadelphia Art Museum and the Enoch Pratt Library in Baltimore speak for themselves.

The combined libraries of Megalopolis, for instance, contain some 100 million volumes. That is one third of the number in the whole United States.

Book publishing too, is all but exclusively concentrated in Megalopolis. A few book publishers are located elsewhere, and college and university presses are scattered across the country. But editors, authors and book salesmen tend to gravitate towards New York.

This concentration of skills, learning and talent, which, of course, goes hand in hand with the concentration of educational and cultural institutions, also attracts the foundations which support so much of our research, education, culture and charity.

### The key to this concentration is skilled and educated people.

There are, as we have seen, few natural resources which would account for this snowballing of services and functions in one small part of the country. Nor does the historic head start account for all of it.

A more important factor is human organization. It is a fact that government, finance, corporation management and all manner of educational, research and cultural institutions require more or less highly trained and specialized employees.

The presence and activities of these people and their organizations, in turn, produce more trained and specialized personnel. And this, again, spawns more institutions and organizations or draws them to Megalopolis.

### An often gaudy, often dismal ugliness

pervades much of Megalopolis, as it does many an American Main Street. There are the beer cans on the highway, the billboards and the jazzy, Disneyland roadside stands and motels. In many of its cities the air is no longer clean. The noise is deafening. The water is polluted. Traffic and transportation are becoming a nightmare. Slums and "grey areas" continue to spread.

Yet, despite these much-criticized facts, the crowded people of Megalopolis are extremely fortunate. They form, on the average, the richest, best-educated, best-housed and best-serviced group of similar size in the world.

13

# Prometheus Unbound

The soaring skylines of Megalopolitan cities are a symbol of their drive and spirit. Less than 300 years after these cities were founded, their skyscrapers ushered in a new era of affluence, of reaching higher and higher. They truly scrape the sky as Prometheus did in the ancient legend.

This giant, according to the Greeks, endeavored to master the secrets of the gods. He stole fire from the sky for man to use.

Most of the settlers who founded America's first cities probably never heard of Prometheus and his exploits. Yet the pioneer spirit which helped them overcome the hardships of the wilderness may well be called Promethean.

The settlers came in the service of such commercial enterprises as the Virginia Company, the Company of the Massachusetts Bay and the Dutch West India Company. These enterprises sought profit. But the men and women they brought over here sought religious freedom as well. They were imbued with a sense of mission, with a spirit quite different from that in which other areas of the world were civilized.

**This spirit set the stage for later immigrants**

who followed the early settlers in much greater numbers. Most of the leaders of the American Revolution built on this Promethean tradition.

It is strikingly expressed by the Great Seal of the United States which shows an *unfinished* pyramid surrounded by two Latin mottos: *Annuit Coeptis* meaning "God Has Favored the Undertaking" and *Novus Ordo Seclorum* meaning "The New Order of the Ages."

Although we don't notice it often, we carry this motto with us on every dollar bill. And we still believe that America does create a new order of the ages by transforming the wilderness into civilization and by creating, on this continent at least, a bastion of freedom and justice. We still insist that Americans can and will make America a better place to live than any other in the world.

Most of us are also still sure that God will reward our toil and daring with material blessings of affluence and progress. The pagan Greeks saw it differently. According to their legend Prometheus was punished for his daring. Zeus chained him to the top of a mountain and sent vultures to feed on his liver.

The meaning of this legend may be that men and societies who steal the fire from the skies with their drive and energy must pay a penalty. Progress seems to bring with it a sense of frustration and constant dissatisfaction. There seems no end to the new problems brought on by the solution of old ones. We are certainly not happy with our mastery of fire power and nuclear energy. Horrible vultures cloud this great promise.

But the promise is there, as is the promise of Megalopolis, a titanic endeavor still a-building. And Megalopolis is unique not only because of geographic location but also because of the Promethean spirit of its people.

# 2 THE ECONOMIC HINGE

Throughout her history America has alternately opened her economic door to world trade and closed it again to concentrate on her internal development. The hinges of this door were the port cities of Megalopolis. They alone had the capital, skill and authority to determine the course of the economy and to profit by it. This hinge position became Megalopolis' economic destiny.

As early as the seventeenth century the new seaboard cities of America had already spun such an elaborate network of trade relationships all over the world that the old ports of England were worried by the competition.

This growth naturally created ever more jobs and ever greater opportunities for anyone willing to work hard. It occurred right at the gate through which came the great flow of immigrants who settled the continent and formed the American nation. Many of them stayed to swell the port cities and to form growing labor and consumer markets.

The skill, energy and aspirations of these people, in turn, further snowballed Megalopolis' stupendous growth.

15

# On the Edge of Wilderness

Most of the early settlers, as we have seen, believed that they had a divine mission in the new country. But their sponsors—the seventeenth century courts and councils of northwestern Europe—hoped for great riches in the newly discovered lands.

The new world was to yield assets the old was lacking. Perhaps a Northwest Passage would be found near the early colonies, leading to the spices of the East Indies. Here, furthermore, was a base of operations that would permit England and the Netherlands to participate in the trade and privateering that had developed in the Caribbean and the West Indies.

And settlement of the new lands, it was hoped, would open up new markets and new sources of supply for European manufacturers and merchants. With these aims in mind, the king in London generously handed out large land grants in the wilderness to favorites such as William Penn and Lord Baltimore.

Similar grants were made in Amsterdam to Dutch nobles of whom the Van Rensselaers are, perhaps, best remembered. Even today the power and wealth associated with these families add lustre to many place names throughout Megalopolis.

The mineral wealth of the new lands quickly disappointed the settlers, who could not forget the glittering piles of gold and silver found in Peru and Mexico.

**There were compensations for the lack of treasure**

in the early colonies. The fur trade was probably the most significant early venture. North American pelts were highly valued in Europe, and Dutch, English and French settlers hunted the animals or obtained their furs from Indians.

The forest stands of New England, New York and Pennsylvania provided much-needed timber for western Europe. Tall trees which could be used for the masts of ships were especially welcome. And so were planks and boards, shingles and clapboards, staves, headings and wine casks.

Some of these wood products were soon also sold to the Caribbean, Madeira, and more distant places. Yankee wood and Yankee ingenuity even anticipated the modern prefabricated house. Whole ready-to-assemble house frames were shipped to the West Indies.

The sea also offered a lucrative harvest in the early years of the colonies. The fishermen of eastern Massachusetts made fortunes on the Grand Banks off Newfoundland, which were teeming with codfish. Dried cod found a thriving market in the West Indies, in the southern colonies and in southern Europe.

A little later, whalers set out to sea from Southampton, New York, and from Nantucket and New Bedford, Massachusetts. Their catch furnished whale oil, which, at the time, lit the lamps of the colonies and of a large part of Europe.

Quebec

Indian Territory

Salem
Boston
Newport
New London
New Haven
New York
Philadelphia
Baltimore

Norfolk

Charleston

Shipping

Whaling

Fishing

Lumbering

Shipbuilding

Iron Works

Grain

Fur trapping

Cotton

Tobacco

**The Economy of the Colonies**

### The produce of the land was of lesser importance

than the produce of the sea. Virginia early developed the cultivation and curing of tobacco, markets for which expanded rapidly. Pennsylvania and New York grew grain and flour in sufficient abundance for export, particularly to the West Indies. But while their agriculture supported the people of the northern and middle colonies, it never became profitable enough to account for the relatively rapid growth of their cities and their financial wealth.

For within a generation or two of their founding, Boston, New York and Philadelphia grew from small port towns into what, by the standards of their time, were large metropolitan cities. By 1775 Philadelphia had, after London, become the largest city in the British Empire.

1690     1775
Boston

1690     1775
Newport

This was not the slow growth of towns which serve only as market places for a farming population. These cities were not even particularly dependent on, or interested in, the land of the Algonquin Indians to their west. They refused to be satisfied with local trade but concentrated largely on overseas commerce.

### The towns of the southern colonies

did not share this mercantile interest and ambition. To the motherland the southern plantations were far more valuable economically. England gained large quantities of tobacco and naval stores, such as tar, pitch, and turpentine. But these products were shipped not from burgeoning port towns but directly from industrial wharves scattered along bays and rivers.

Thus the only important city to develop in the South in colonial times was Charleston in South Carolina. By 1760 Charleston reached the size of 8,000 inhabitants, while Boston already came close to reaching twice, New York three times and Philadelphia four times that number.

The northern colonies, in contrast, had little to offer England, aside from furs and masts. Yankee merchants and seamen therefore had to use their ingenious "triangular" routes of trade to make profits.

### Determined "to trye all ports,"

as they put it, they would take flour from Philadelphia and New York, horses and cattle from Connecticut, and dried fish and lumber from Massachusetts to the West Indies. They exchanged these cargoes for sugar, indigo or coffee and carried them to England. From there they would take various manufactures back to America.

In another such triangle, ships from Newport would shuttle between Rhode Island, the West African coast and the West Indies, trading Negro slaves for molasses, which converted into rum, could be exchanged for more slaves.

Still other trade routes, not all of them legal under the English Navigation Acts, took Yankee ships to the French and Spanish islands in the Caribbean and to the ports of Europe. They returned from there with wine and salt.

Fishing, whaling and trading required ships, of course, and these the colonies built themselves. As early as 1710 twenty-one ships, totalling 1,520 tons, were launched in Massachusetts. The first schooner was built in Boston in 1716. Seven years later New England

New York

Philadelphia

Charleston

1690 1775

1690 1775

1690 1775

launched 700 ships. London looked upon the well-managed shipbuilding industry across the Atlantic with envy and some concern.

This industry employed the skills of the many craftsmen and arti-
sans who were among the first settlers of Massachusetts, New Amsterdam and, later, Philadelphia. William Penn, in 1685, boasted of the
many useful tradesmen in his city. Among them were carpenters,
wheelwrights, shipwrights, shoemakers and ropemakers. Boston at
around that time already supported 24 silversmiths, a sign of of considerable urban sophistication.

And the skill of the craftsmen combined with that of the traders
soon built up substantial capital in the big seaports. Most of it was
invested locally, either in more trade and ships or in more graceful
living, real estate and manufactures, and in land speculation farther
in the interior.

### A wealthy elite of proud and powerful townspeople

thus arose. And so did increasing rivalry between the spreading cities,
particularly between Boston and New York.

By the middle of the eighteenth century things began to change
somewhat. The Treaty of Utrecht, in 1713, had brought peace on
land and sea, spurring both further maritime commerce and inland
expansion. More immigrants arrived, not only Englishmen but Scots,
Irish, French Huguenots, Swiss and Germans as well.

The latter settled mostly in the middle colonies with their greater
religious tolerance and abundance of free land. The "Pennsylvania
Dutch" country was settled. Baltimore surpassed the older Annapolis
and became another important market center and seaport. It was also
a convenient stopping point on the overland route as land traffic began
to rival the waterways.

### On the eve of the American revolution

the area of Megalopolis held about three-fifths of the total three million population of the colonies. Many new towns had been founded,
supported by ever increasing commerce, industry and agriculture.

Yet the colonies felt restless and hemmed in; first, by the French
outposts, and later, by British attempts to curb both internal expansion and overseas trade. The French and Indian Wars and the defeat
of France in Europe broke the first barrier. The second exploded with
the Boston Tea Party and the revolution against taxation without
representation.

# From Saratoga to Waterloo

With the Revolutionary War won and independence achieved, the American people took their destinies into their own hands.

And the remarkable forty years that followed—years of excitement, adventure, profits and expansion—saw the nuclei of today's Megalopolis taking firm shape.

True, the march to the West had begun. By 1790 there were already a respectable number of settlers in Kentucky and Tennessee and in the Ohio Valley around Pittsburgh.

By 1810 the center of population of the United States was west of the Potomac, just a little south of Charlestown, Maryland. By 1820 it had shifted to a point just west of the present border between Virginia and West Virginia. The purchase of Louisiana further helped to make the development of the country's interior a major endeavor for the American people.

But immediately after the Revolution and a brief period of reconstruction, the economic emphasis of the northwestern states shifted once more toward the sea.

### The economic doors of the United States

opened even wider toward the vast opportunities of maritime trade. And this, in turn, gave the cities on the hinge an added stimulus for urban growth.

Megalopolis established its economic supremacy in the new nation. It retained this position even when after the War of 1812, the doors swung west for a while toward internal expansion.

The success of America's first great overseas enterprise was all the more remarkable because the Revolutionary War had, of course disrupted the triangular navigation within and around the British Empire.

But in the "trye all ports" tradition, privateering, practiced earlier during the wars with Spain and France (1744-83), was revived during the Revolutionary War, this time against English ships.

While British ports remained closed to them, Americans continued their trade with the British West Indies via the French and Spanish islands. Americans supplied much of the food for the slaves working on the French and Spanish sugar plantations.

### The promising China trade

was opened in 1784 by the *Empress of China*. At home in New York, built in Baltimore, managed by a Boston firm, and financed by Philadelphians, she was truly a Megalopolitan ship.

Other ships soon followed. In 1787 Captain Robert Gray of Boston sailed to the estuary of the Columbia River in the Pacific Northwest and found it teeming with seals and sea otters. Knowing that the Chinese highly valued the pelts of these animals, he took them to Canton and returned to Boston with tea. Another triangle—Boston, Pacific Northwest and China—was inaugurated.

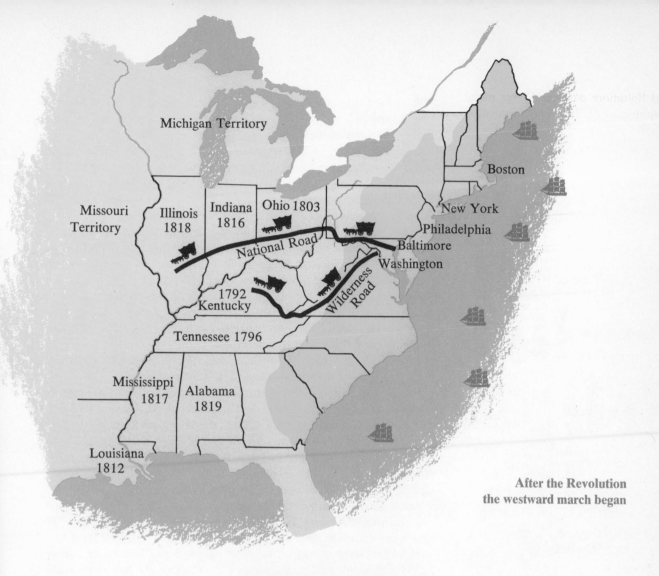

Michigan Territory

Missouri Territory

Illinois 1818

Indiana 1816

Ohio 1803

National Road

1792 Kentucky

Tennessee 1796

Mississippi 1817

Alabama 1819

Louisiana 1812

Wilderness Road

Boston

New York

Philadelphia

Baltimore

Washington

After the Revolution
the westward march began

### American shipping and shipyards

both received another boost when, in 1789, Congress established entrance duties at U.S. ports. Foreign-built and -owned ships had to pay fifty cents per ton, while American-built ships paid thirty cents if foreign-owned and only six cents if owned by Americans.

### War in Europe further helped

the tremendous maritime boom. From 1792 to 1815 France dominated the European continent and she and Britain remained almost constantly at war, trying to blockade one another. The United States made good use of its neutrality as well of its favorable geographic position on the Atlantic.

American ships could sail where the belligerents dared not. The Americans risked seizures and other complications, of course, but the profits were great.

When the British started to interfere with U.S. vessels carrying sugar from the West Indies to Europe, the ships simply broke the voyage at some American port. U.S. trade statistics became suddenly inflated with the entry and quick withdrawal of hundreds of such cargoes. It was an easy way to make money.

21

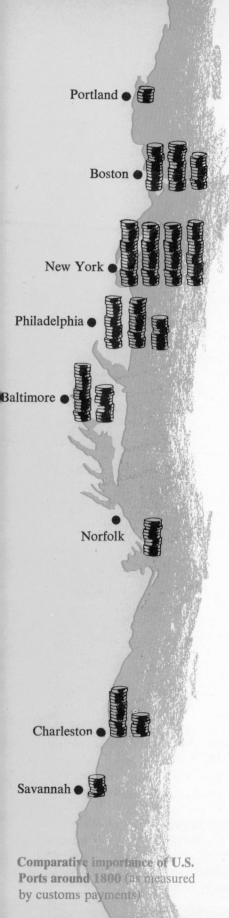

Comparative importance of U.S.
Ports around 1800 (as measured
by customs payments)

The boom continued until 1807. Then there was a period of ups and downs affected by the uncertain political situation in Europe and particularly by worsening British-American relations.

President Jefferson first imposed an embargo on all foreign trade and then softened it to "nonintercourse" with France and England. But he could not prevent the War of 1812, which brought the British to the northeastern seaboard. For a while it was unsafe for American vessels to trade even in the Long Island Sound.

When peace was restored, Napoleon had been defeated at Waterloo and the European powers returned to normal trade. Its opportunities on the seas thus limited, Megalopolis shifted its economic emphasis from foreign commerce to domestic manufacturing.

But the maritime fling had paid off for both the nation in general and for Megalopolis in particular. National wealth had more than doubled. The size of the merchant marine had tripled. Foreign trade had expanded three and a half times.

New York now took the definite lead among American seaports, largely because of the spaciousness of its harbor.

Boston had suffered during the troubles preceding the Revolutionary War, but, by 1791, it had more than recovered. On one October day of that year over seventy vessels sailed out of its harbor. And soon its tonnage was second only to that of New York.

A Boston specialty in those days was the export of ice, cut on the frozen lakes and packed in pine sawdust. It cooled the drinks of the rich of the West Indies and as far away as Brazil.

Immediately after the Revolution, Philadelphia was both the largest city and busiest seaport. New York surpassed it in commerce in 1797 and in population around 1810.

Baltimore ranked fourth. It owed its rapid rise less to its harbor facilities than to its inland location on the Chesapeake Bay. This made it easily accessible to the exports from plantations and small towns along the indented coast to which, in turn, it redistributed imports such as sugar from the West Indies or hardware from Europe.

During the War this location was also considered a safe deposit for capital, out of reach of enemy raids. Baltimore was among the earliest manufacturing cities. In 1797 it claimed the first umbrella made in America.

### Washington,

of course, was a newcomer to the northeastern seaboard cities. Its founders hoped the Federal city on the Potomac would become another great center of commerce and industry. But these hopes came to nothing and until recently Washington's population and cultural growth were entirely dependent on its function as the seat of the national government.

Yet this fact alone made Washington an important southern "joint" of the hinge. As the center of domestic and foreign policy it added a political element to the hinge function of Megalopolis. If nothing else, the other Megalopolitan cities were now closer to the Federal government than other important cities elsewhere in the United States.

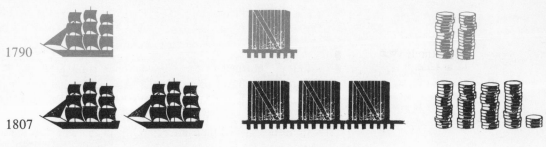

1790

1807

Gross Tonnage of Merchant Marine     Foreign Trade     National Wealth

### Numerous small seaboard towns

also benefited from their hinge function and grew rapidly during this period. Some of them challenged the "pull" of the large centers by developing specialties of their own. Thus some New England towns, like Salem, Gloucester and Provincetown, concentrated on cod fishing. Others, notably Nantucket and New Bedford, favored whaling, while the small town of Wethersfield, Connecticut specialized in growing onions on a large scale and sold them not only in the nearby cities but also in the far-away West Indies.

### Not all Americans welcomed urban growth,

however, even then. Thomas Jefferson, representing the agrarian South, distrusted the mercantile interests of the large northeastern cities. He was, in fact, against cities as such and opposed the industrialization and urbanization of the United States.

"Let our workshops remain in Europe," was his favorite phrase. His views were reminiscent of Plato's *Laws*. For the Greek philosopher, too, wanted to protect Athens from the mercantile interests and the political views of agitated seamen. Plato's ideal republic was to be on an isolated island, a distance away from the seashore. He wanted matters of foreign relations and sea trade attended to by a small number of expert public servants.

Hamilton, in contrast, vigorously advocated the development of trade and manufacturing for the new Republic. He was one of the founders and a director of the first bank established in New York City in 1784. And he was among the leaders of the great maritime expansion of his period.

In the end, Jefferson relented somewhat in his anti-city attitude and his opposition to industry. In 1785 he had written: "The mobs of great cities add just as much to the support of pure government as sores do to strength of the human body." Thirty-one years later he admitted, however, that "experience has taught me that manufactures are now as necessary to our independence as to our comfort."

He accepted cities as industrial rather than commercial centers, for native American industry seemed to him to limit the danger that mercantile interests might influence foreign policy in favor of "foreign entanglements."

# From the Wharf to the Waterfall

"Normalcy" returned to the United States soon after the War of 1812. But it returned to Europe as well. And as normal trade patterns were reestablished there, American merchants found that the period of big and quick shipping profits was over for a while.

They therefore turned their attention "from the wharf to the waterfall." The phrase originated in New England, but interest in the water-powered textile mills and other manufacturing plants was general throughout the northeastern seaboard.

### A protective tariff

further advanced this trend. Congress passed it in 1816, fearful of the dumping of European manufactures on the American market and determined to build up and protect native American industry.

The country united behind Hamilton's economic policy and later supported the "American System" offered by Henry Clay in a famous speech in March 1824. He called for the development of large industrial cities which would supply the nation with manufactures and the farmers with a consumer market for their products. This would assure both prosperity and economic independence from Europe.

### The new manufacturing plants

sprang up mostly in and around the eastern seaports. There was a sprinkling of diversified factories in the South (Virginia and the Carolina Piedmont), in the Mohawk Valley, and beyond the Appalachians in western Pennsylvania and the Ohio Valley.

But the cities of Megalopolis had, in the first place, a greater build-up of capital to finance new industries. It was here, furthermore, that the greatest number of consumers were concentrated. And it was in the port cities that abundant and cheap immigrant labor as well as machinery and equipment arrived from abroad.

Thus, in the first quarter of the nineteenth century, numerous new textile mills mushroomed in the vicinity of Boston (Waltham and

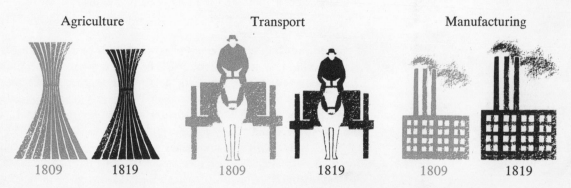

| Agriculture | Transport | Manufacturing |
| --- | --- | --- |
| 1809    1819 | 1809    1819 | 1809    1819 |

After the War of 1812, transport and agriculture drop but manufacturing rises

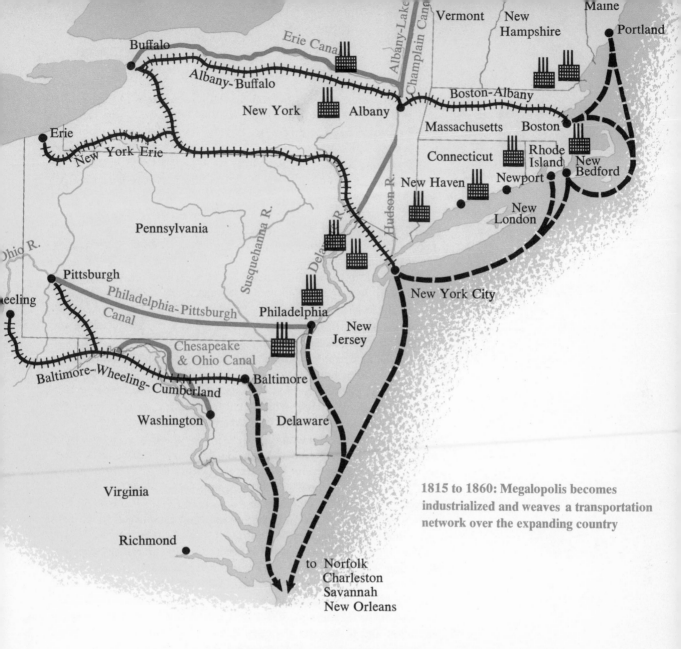

Maine
Portland
Vermont
New Hampshire
Erie Canal
Albany-Lake
Champlain Canal
Buffalo
Albany-Buffalo
Boston-Albany
New York
Albany
Massachusetts
Boston
Connecticut
Rhode Island
New Bedford
New Haven
Newport
New London
New York Erie
Erie
Hudson R.
Pennsylvania
Susquehanna R.
Delaware R.
Ohio R.
Pittsburgh
Philadelphia-Pittsburgh Canal
New York City
Wheeling
Philadelphia
New Jersey
Chesapeake & Ohio Canal
Baltimore-Wheeling- Cumberland
Baltimore
Delaware
Washington

1815 to 1860: Megalopolis becomes industrialized and weaves a transportation network over the expanding country

Virginia

Richmond

to Norfolk
Charleston
Savannah
New Orleans

Lowell), of Providence (Fall River and Pawtucket) and New York (Paterson). A number of Connecticut towns (New Haven, Berlin and Middletown) turned to the manufacture of guns. And the Baldwin Locomotive plant was founded in Philadelphia in 1832.

**Better transportation,**

to supply raw materials and distribute the goods produced, was a foremost need of the new factories. The seaboard South could communicate with the great northeastern ports by coastwise navigation. But the developing regions along the Ohio River, the upper Mississippi and the Great Lakes might well have looked downstream toward New Orleans if adequate waterway links to New York, Philadelphia and Baltimore had not been provided.

Since all three cities vied for their trade, an interesting race began in the 1820's.

25

Boston

New York

Philadelphia

Baltimore

**Relative importance of U.S. Ports in 1860**
(in dollar value of foreign trade)

Mobile

New Orleans

In Baltimore and Washington the idea of a canal linking Chesapeake Bay with the Ohio Valley via the Potomac Valley and the Cumberland Gap was first advanced by the Patowmack Company, whose president was none other than George Washington.

New York, in 1825, triumphantly inaugurated the Erie Canal, begun in 1817. It linked Buffalo, on Lake Erie, with the Hudson River at Albany by way of the Mohawk Valley.

Outflanking Niagara Falls on reaching Lake Erie, this canal established a water route from as far as Lake Michigan to New York harbor. Water transportation at the time was, of course, far less expensive than transport by wagon.

Another canal was constructed from Albany northward to Lake Champlain. New York thus put to excellent use its geographic location at the foot of a strategic "Y".

But the Great Lakes region was not yet as well developed as was the Ohio Valley at the time. This caused Philadelphia, in 1826, to start building a canal system to Pittsburgh and the Ohio. A special rail link was devised to carry cargo across the Appalachians.

This canal opened in 1834. But its operation proved more expensive than the Erie Canal, which, ten years later, carried almost five times as much freight as the Pennsylvania Main Line Canal.

The Chesapeake and Ohio Canal, too, was unable to compete. Baltimore merchants preferred to push the new and more efficient mode of rail transportation. In 1850, in the words of one historian, the much-delayed canal finally "staggered into Cumberland on the upper Potomac eight years behind the Baltimore and Ohio Railroad."

New York had thus won the canal race and established its primacy as a seaport and transportation hub.

The puffing iron horses soon made the canals altogether obsolete. Railroads moved freight faster—twenty-five miles an hour!—would not freeze in winter, and could span hills and plains alike.

Once again Megalopolis moved rapidly to exploit the new development. It financed the network of railroads that was soon to cover the continent and to become the country's major business.

And once again New York emerged as the leader.

As the 1830's and the Jackson era came close, tariffs were lowered again but a financial crisis developed. The banks in Manhattan, having more skill and capital than others, united to deal with the crisis. As a result New York recovered more quickly from the panic of 1837 than Philadelphia and the South, and thus won the race for leadership in banking as well as in transportation.

### A new era of prosperity

began with the "roaring forties" both in Europe and America. The economic doors swung once again toward the sea. The United States increased its exports of grain, flour, tobacco, cotton and even manufactured goods to a rapidly industrializing Europe and developed new markets in Latin America. Foreign trade rose more rapidly from 1843 to 1860 than income from manufacturing or the national income.

1830 - 1840

1840 - 1850

1850 - 1860

Immigration 1820 to 1860

Boston, New York, and Baltimore developed large metal smelting and refining plants. The Naugatuck Valley in Connecticut specialized in textiles. Rhode Island, too, developed a successful, large-scale cotton textile industry. Cotton and wool textile factories spread to Massachusetts and then southward to New Jersey and the region of Philadelphia. Later New York became the capital of the clothing industry.

Arms manufacturing began in New England with Eli Whitney and Simeon North, and this led to the manufacture of other precision machinery, including clocks. Footwear and woodenware factories were also established.

Pennsylvania led in making glassware, paper, iron, and some types of heavy machinery. Wilmington became the headquarters of du Pont's gunpowder and chemical industry. Baltimore led the country in canning.

Boston, New York, Philadelphia and Baltimore now fancied themselves "ports of the world." From them, starting around 1850, sailed the fastest sailing ships ever built, the famous "clippers." They were speedy schooners, able to dodge foreign patrols at sea and to maneuver easily when approaching land. In 1851 the specially built 100-foot clipper *America* won the yacht race around the Isle of Wight, the first of the America's Cup races.

The *Flying Cloud* made it from New York to San Francisco in 89 days. The gold rush to California had made the routes from New York and Boston to San Francisco among the most travelled of the sea lanes. Freight to the west coast went around the Horn, the long way. Passengers and mail went by sea to the Isthmus of Panama, overland across it, and again by sea along the Pacific shores. In 1855 American capital built a railroad across the Isthmus to accelerate the trip.

### Shipbuilding

prospered as never before and about 80 per cent of the nation's vessels were built in New England. The American merchant marine nearly surpassed the British in peaceful, cordial competition. Yankee clippers challenged the British on the silk and tea trade and on the Australian routes.

But, proud of their sailing ships, American shipbuilders did not pay sufficient attention to the iron-built steamers the British and other Europeans were using increasingly. As a result American shipping, by 1860, fell behind again.

The clippers and maritime ventures, however, made the money which Megalopolis invested in the development of the continent.

### Immigrants

further swelled the traffic in the ports. The bad crops and famine in Ireland and the aftermath of the European revolutions of 1848 brought ever increasing tides of people. The record year of 1854 saw an influx of nearly half a million immigrants, a figure not to be equalled again until 1873. The population of the larger northeastern cities increased even faster than before. After 1850 the rate of growth accelerated in Newark and Jersey City, New Jersey, and Worcester, Massachusetts.

But Detroit and Chicago also expanded enormously. For not all the immigrants stayed in Megalopolis.

### Prairie farming

came into its own after 1850. Up until then the typical American pioneer was the backwoodsman. Settlement was all but limited to the forests and the smaller prairies where there was wood and water. The large, treeless expanses of Illinois and Iowa were devoid of shelter and remote from markets.

This changed when the McCormick family came to Chicago and launched a big industry producing agricultural machinery. And the railroad network began to penetrate the Great Plains.

Expanded demand for agricultural produce sped the development of the Midwest. There were millions more people to feed now along the eastern seaboard. And Britain and France, cut off from the Ukrainian breadbasket by the Crimean War with Russia, also imported more American foodstuffs.

### Eastern banks financed the inland progress,

or much of it. National credit and money management was concentrated in the four large cities of Megalopolis. Banks were, of course, established all over the expanded United States. But they all needed "correspondents" in the east, preferably New York and Boston.

There were several reasons for this concentration. Country banks had surplus funds during harvest time while at other times they needed to borrow. Only the large seaports had large banks which had to make many payments for exports and imports all year around. To maintain balances in them gave good national standing to the notes of smalltown banks. And the larger markets had better rates.

Businessmen in the small mill towns, moreover, felt that local banks might be too readily influenced by local circumstances or their own financial difficulties. The big city banks, on the other hand, had, of course, many similar or larger accounts and enough resources to cope with any situation but a national panic.

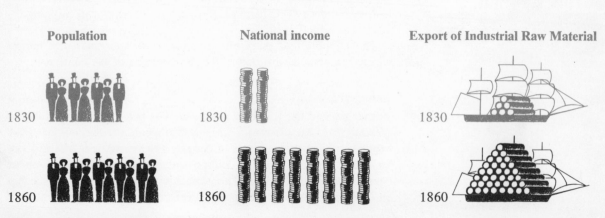

Population     National income     Export of Industrial Raw Material

1830    1830    1830

1860    1860    1860

As industry developed elsewhere, Megalopolis concentrated on commerce and management

# After Appomattox

The Civil War naturally disrupted foreign maritime relations but gave a great boost to manufacturing. In the end, the big cities of the victorious North had the task of directing and financing the reconstruction of the South as well as the great westward expansion from the Mississippi to the Pacific.

Megalopolis was thus confirmed as the economic manager of the whole nation.

Foreign trade declined in the 1860's. So did the tonnage of the merchant marine as many American vessels were sold to foreigners who could enjoy neutrality in all American ports.

Nor did shipping resume significantly when the fighting was over. Megalopolitan merchants could now maintain overseas commerce by transatlantic cable. They found 4 or 5 per cent profit on shipping far less attractive than the 6 to 10 per cent gain promised by exploitation of the West. The great empire builders soon fought their famous battles for control of the railroads. Following on the heels of the pioneers and their covered wagons, the railways were the major tool for the organization of the wide open spaces. In 1869 the Union Pacific and the Central Pacific joined at Promontory Point, Utah, and the dream of a transcontinental railroad became a reality.

Capital invested in the railroads themselves and in various businesses connected with developing the lands along the lines increased about 500 times from 1867 to 1880. This investment almost doubled again by 1890. Railroad stocks and bonds dominated the stock exchanges, primarily Wall Street. And a fierce rivalry to attract rail freight and passengers developed between the large cities.

**The railroads fought a bitter rate warfare**

in the 1870's and 1880's, greatly lowering transportation cost to inland cities. Rates from New York to Chicago per hundred pounds of grain went down from sixty cents in 1873 to thirty cents in 1875. Baltimore and Philadelphia tried to undersell New York, going down to twenty cents. In 1876 a carload of cattle could be moved from Chicago to New York for one dollar. Immigrant passengers, too, paid only a dollar per head for the trip. The Baltimore and Ohio and the Erie lines were near bankruptcy but continued to fight.

The rate war frustrated New Orleans' attempt to attract a greater share of the business to the Mississippi. It hurt the Erie Canal, too. But low rail transportation cost and the fierce competition between its cities vastly benefited Megalopolis as a whole. Its bankers could always make up in foreign trade what they occasionally lost by drastic cuts in rail rates. They also channeled a substantial amount of foreign capital into American railroad investment. In 1907 one quarter, and in 1914 one third, of all railroad stocks and bonds were held abroad.

Corruption and scandals, and the Granger movement, forced increasing Federal regulation of the railroads. Farmers, particularly in the Southeast, bitterly complained that rates discriminated against them. But no amount of regulation could change the basic fact that Megalopolis had logically developed into the densest transportation hub in the nation and thus had the most competitive rates. It handled export and import and had the greatest concentration of people, of purchasing power and of diversified manufacturing.

**Heavy industry moved West,**

on or near the coal and iron deposits between the Ohio Valley and the Great Lakes. Some lighter industries began to move southward. And at the turn of the century some midwestern cities, notably Chicago, Pittsburgh and Cleveland, seemed to be taking on some independence as regional metropolises.

The northern industrial Midwest now grew at a faster rate than Megalopolis. It looked as though leadership might transfer to the heart of the continent. It became popular to contend that New York was not really America while Chicago certainly was.

**Foreign affairs,**

however, kept the hinge swinging. And the hinge function continued to keep Megalopolis in the lead. New interests abroad began to assert themselves early in the present century. The Spanish-American War involved the United States in Puerto Rico, Cuba, and the

Philippines. Theodore Roosevelt's policies expanded the American stakes in Latin America.

Although close to economic self-sufficiency, America's agricultural prosperity needed large exports. The country also exported many industrial raw materials and imported numerous other commodities. It thus could no longer remain disinterested in international affairs that affected its major markets abroad.

This interest projected the United States into the position of mediator at international conferences, such as the Portsmouth Treaty ending the Russian-Japanese conflict in 1905 and the Algeciras Conference on Morocco in 1906.

By the time World War I interrupted half a century of internal growth and development, the country had, furthermore, become largely a nation of cities. Evidence of its urban pursuits was the fact that in every year after 1880 the income from trade, transportation and services combined exceeded that from either manufacturing or agriculture.

At first the Middle West cared little about the holocaust in faraway Europe. But Megalopolis immediately sensed its powerful im-

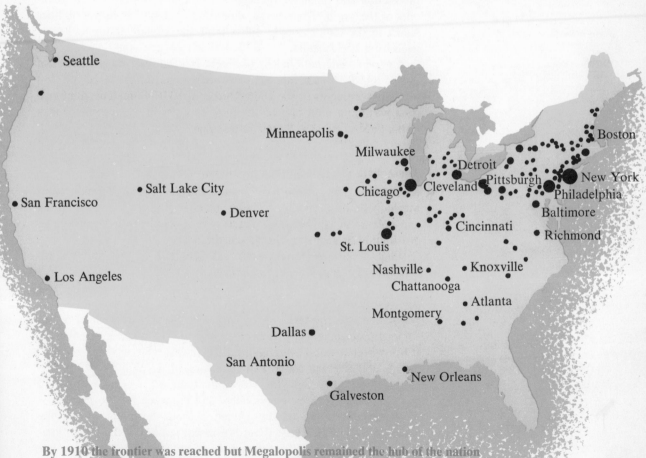

By 1910 the frontier was reached but Megalopolis remained the hub of the nation

Boston

Providence

New Haven

New York

Philadelphia

Baltimore

Inbound and outbound shipments in Megalopolitan ports

pact on the American destiny. The two World Wars engaged the United States more actively than ever in the affairs of the world. And both times the end of the conflict found the United States the only power able to replenish the resources of the other belligerents.

### The United States became the creditor of the world,

and this new function is still concentrated in Megalopolis. The chief seat of international banking is New York City. There has been some decentralization toward Washington, where the Federal financial institutions and, since 1947, the World Bank and the International Monetary Fund are located. Boston and Philadelphia share a decreasing role in international financial activities.

For a short period between the World Wars, from 1925 to 1938, domestic preoccupations dominated the American economy. The prosperity of the late 1920's and the great depression that followed were not confined to the United States, although it was here that the contrast was sharpest.

But the stupendous growth of American consumption, reflecting the rise both in population and in standard of living, soon built up production and financing on such a scale that it dominated the economy of the world. This offered opportunities as well as responsibilities which made it increasingly difficult for the United States to isolate itself from world affairs.

America's international involvement is illustrated by the fact that in 1957 U.S. investments abroad were estimated at $54 billion and foreign investments in the United States at $31 billion. The combined total was more than half of the total deposits in the member banks of the Federal Reserve System in that year.

### The growth of cities became less important

after 1914. This period saw a good deal of decentralization from Megalopolis in terms of population numbers, value of manufacturing and volume of consumption. There was a trend toward more equal distribution of all three throughout the nation.

What became important now was suburban sprawl and the redistribution of functions within Megalopolis itself.

For the area retained not only a good deal of manufacturing and services in its enormous market made up of one-fifth of the nation's population and two-fifths of its bank deposits. It also retained or developed specializations that have preserved its wealth and influence. It has woven a web of interconnections, measurable in terms of automobile and airplane traffic and frequency of telephone calls, that is more complex and highly developed than any other in the nation. All this offers more profits, employment and influence for the future.

The establishment of the United Nations headquarters on the banks of New York's East River is a recent symbol of the hinge function of Megalopolis. That function helps us understand the phenomenal growth of Megalopolis in the past. It remains the key to its present and future dynamics.

32

# 3 WHY CITIES GROW
## AND SUBURBS SCATTER

The first villages in the North American colonies were built in the years 1625 to 1650.

By 1690, five of them had become respectable towns. Four of these —Boston with 7,000 inhabitants, Newport with 2,600, New York with 3,000 and Philadelphia with 4,000—were in what is today Megalopolis. The fifth, Charleston, had some 1,100 people.

When the Revolutionary War broke out, Boston had more than doubled and Newport quadrupled. New York's population had increased eight times and Philadelphia's more than ten times. Five additional towns with over 5,000 inhabitants dotted the map of Megalopolis—Salem, New Haven, Norwich, New London, and Baltimore. Two more, Charleston and Norfolk, had risen in the South.

There were also eight townships in Massachusetts and Connecticut of about 5,000 population. These were not strictly speaking "towns" but consisted, rather, of small groups of residences or of one very small town surrounded by a scattering of farmsteads on the township territory.

There was good reason why New England had more towns than the rest of the country. The founding fathers of Massachusetts did not officially allow settlers to claim land and settle it by themselves, as was done in Virginia.

Puritan society believed in organizing communities, as these were better able to practice religion than were isolated individuals. Towns, furthermore, were easier to police and to defend and offered better opportunities for education. Their inhabitants shared communal land, the common pasture, which developed into the New England Commons, or village green. This helped the small farmer who had suffered because of the breaking up of just such common lands in England.

Last but not least, the town proprietors who were granted or had purchased New England townships, could profit more, of course, if they kept their colonists together.

Some settlers did, however, break away from the townships both in individual families and in larger groups. Their reasons were manifold. Often it was a desire for greater independence and social and economic freedom. Just as often the break had religious motives. And at times the break was caused simply by the lure of adventure in the wilderness.

But the most frequently advanced reason was "a feeling of crowding"—a reason which continued to be advanced throughout the history of America's urbanization. Crowding is, of course, a subjective matter. People feel crowded when they want change and believe they are entitled to another environment which offers them greater opportunities.

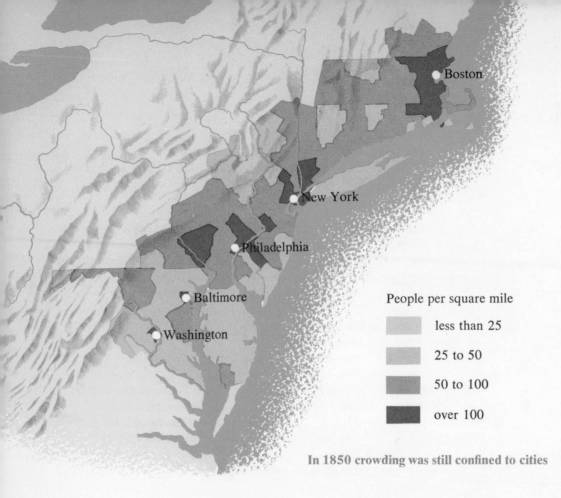

People per square mile

less than 25

25 to 50

50 to 100

over 100

In 1850 crowding was still confined to cities

In any event, whole groups throughout the seventeenth century split away from the Massachusetts townships and started new settlements in Connecticut. And since these new towns offered their citizens greater participation in public affairs they attracted more people and grew faster than the older communities.

Some of the new towns, such as Reading, were laid out in the same manner in which William Penn planned Philadelphia in 1681. He arranged the streets in a gridiron pattern, a layout which thousands of American cities also adopted.

**The motivation for founding new towns varied.**

A good many towns, like Philadelphia and Annapolis, were founded by religious sects wishing to worship in their own way. Thus the Moravians founded Bethlehem. The Mennonites founded Lancaster. Quaker groups established several towns in New Jersey.

These early ports or market places laid the foundation of American urban society. They were provincial centers with many of the conveniences of similar towns in Europe and many of the problems of the small-scale urban life of the time.

And, like cities anywhere, they were well-serviced centers for the exchange of goods and ideas, for the administration of justice and politics, for the celebration of religious rites and other collective tra-

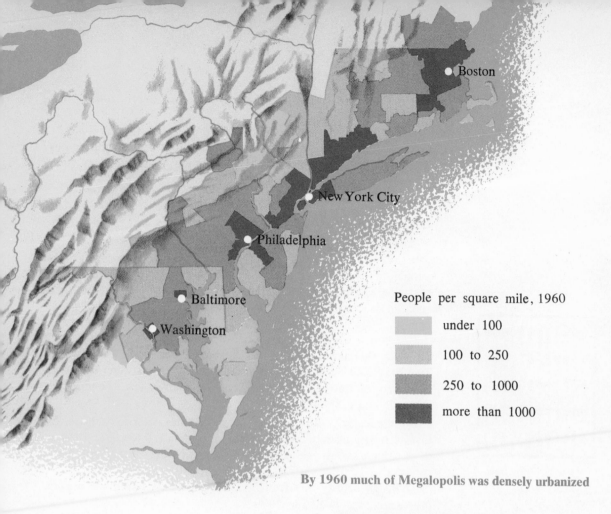

By 1960 much of Megalopolis was densely urbanized

ditions, for education, and for relaxation. Today, in Megalopolis, such centers are merely the "downtown" areas.

Under the pressure of people and activities wishing to locate in or near them, they kept expanding and some of their functions were transferred elsewhere.

### Some centers were planned

for special reasons. But such instances are rare. One example is Washington, D.C., which was planned by Major Pierre Charles L'Enfant as the seat of the national government. The basic concepts of L'Enfant's plan have survived even the motor age. With its grand Mall and wide avenues, radiating from the Capitol, it gives our Federal city its distinct character.

A city planned as a port and industrial city is Baltimore.

In other cases functions hitherto confined to the inner city moved to suburbs. But the growing city often caught up, and they were later again incorporated within the city's legal territory. Other such suburbs became cities in their own right, although they remained in many respects satellites to the centers from which they emanated.

Later, residences, stores and factories scattered to such an extent that entire countryside areas became urbanized.

Such urbanization disperses city activities over the landscape much like colloids in chemistry. The particles are hardly visible and rarely jell. And like the nebulae of the Milky Way this form of urban sprawl has no discernible structure.

The process has also been called "the exploding metropolis," a product of "the urban revolution." The empty seventeenth century wilderness of the northeastern United States thus gave way to an intensely crowded one.

### Dispersal began about 1850.

At that time the map of the Megalopolitan area shows 85 cities with more than 8,000 people, holding 12.5 per cent of the total population. They are naturally concentrated along the main transportation arteries—the seaboard axis of U.S. Route 1 and the roads and canals which radiate out from Boston, New York and Philadelphia.

New towns were still to arise between the Harrisburg-York area in the Susquehanna Valley and the Pittsburgh area in the Ohio Valley. The 1850 map doesn't show them yet because towns were, of course, dependent on transportation and Pennsylvania was late in building its railroads and canal westward.

But the majority of real centers, of what today constitutes the downtown business district, were already in existence. From that time on these centers merely increased their population density, expanded and sprawled.

The high density belt from greater Boston to Baltimore became practically consolidated by 1870.

Some farming areas already began to decrease both in population and in tilled acreage. Farmers deserted their land, lured by the promise of a better life either in the city or on the Western frontier. Urban uses of the land soon filled the vacuum.

The only important change in the external shape of Megalopolis in the past hundred years is that it has grown south to encompass the Washington metropolitan area. This is the result of two new developments at work since 1915: the growth of the activities and economic impact of the Federal government and the economic growth of the Southeast.

### Megalopolis' boundaries remain unchanged.

Internal gaps were filled in and farm areas turned into suburbs or "outer-suburbia." This was particularly true after 1930 when the automobile began to dominate all transportation.

The important development, then, is not an increase in the size of Megalopolis but its ever increasing number of inhabitants and the intensive use to which they put the land.

In 1960 the 53,575 square miles of Megalopolis averaged a population density of 688 people per square mile. This was almost fourteen times more than the national average.

Even if the areas and populations of the five largest cities in Megalopolis are excluded from this total, the average population density of the region is still nine times the national average.

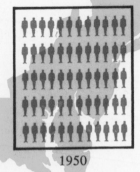

1950

**Increase in population density in Megalopolis**

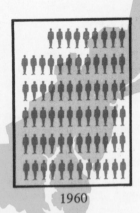

1960

# The Lure of Cities

The enterprise of merchants, bankers and manufacturers who exploited the opportunities of the hinge was not the only thing that attracted people to cities.

There was also the promise of urban living.

Even in colonial times the leading cities of the Northeast had developed a stimulating intellectual life with a diversity of cultural activities and greater political participation and freedom than country living offered.

### The "pull" of the city and the "push" off the farm

often coincided. Boston and New York, for instance, pulled the immigrants who were pushed off the Irish land during the 1840-1860 famine.

Nor was the migration to the cities all from abroad. Since the middle of the nineteenth century farmers have been deserting their land in all industrialized countries. Machines, better seeds and fertilizers replaced many of these farm hands.

In the United States farms abandoned at that time can still be seen from Maine to Virginia. The fields are overgrown with brush, and untended fruit trees suddenly bloom in the woods. Dense underbrush has swallowed crumbling stone walls and even buildings.

The owners of these deserted farms flocked to the more promising life of the city with its opportunities for education and better income. Others migrated to larger, more profitable farms beyond the Appalachians.

The hinge position of Megalopolis involved the exchange not only of goods but also of people. While immigrants kept arriving from overseas, the northeastern states continued to send people out west.

The northern New England states, for instance, lost more people between 1870 and 1950 than came in. Pennsylvania, suffering the decline of its coal mining areas, barely kept its balance.

### At the end of the 19th century

a more positive attitude towards the city began to emerge in America. Following Jefferson's lead, American intellectuals—notably Thoreau, Emerson and Henry Adams—expressed themselves generally as anti-city. Pro-city exceptions were Benjamin Franklin, Alexander Hamilton and Walt Whitman.

This anti-city attitude has complex roots. There has been and still is an aesthetic reaction against the drabness and ugliness of the city, its slums, industrial smoke and stench. There is also ethical disapproval of mixing so much obvious poverty with such ostentatious wealth and of the regimentation necessitated by close living together.

There is, furthermore, a moralistic disdain of the demagoguery and corruption of city hall. This combines with a vague faith in the greater democratic virtues of the country squire and the notion that

Average population density per square mile: U.S.

life on the bosom of mother nature is more healthful and virtuous than in the corrupted and "artificial" urban environment.

To this day these concepts view the city as evil and degrading, and call for housing people in the open country as a matter of human redemption and salvation.

Not all this thinking has been harmful to the inevitable development of cities. It is regrettable that their disgust for State Street kept people like Emerson, Henry Adams, Henry James and their followers from trying to improve Boston's politics and government. But eventually this attitude did help bring about many improvements in city housing, water supply, public health and labor legislation.

Thoreau not only eulogized the romantic wilderness. He also took the trouble to advocate large parks in every city. Later generations followed his advice.

The anti-city philosophers thus inspired many of the greatly needed social reforms of the late nineteenth century. They planted the seeds for the progressive movements, led by Theodore Roosevelt and Woodrow Wilson, which set out to meet the problems of modern, urban-industrial culture in America.

Simultaneously Americans began thinking about the conservation of the beauty and the spiritual and material resources of their countryside. Through the efforts of George P. Marsh, Frederick L. Olmsted, Gifford Pinchot and others, the national and state governments began at last to conserve forests and create public parks.

Olmsted won the competition for the design of Central Park in Manhattan in 1858. Five years later he resigned as its chief architect, discouraged by the constant struggle this splendidly far-sighted project involved. Yet, in 1882 Olmsted was still working on such parks in fifteen American cities.

### Social reform has added to the urban crowding.

New York's mayor Fiorello La Guardia testified in 1940: "Now, cities that are more human than others are penalized for it, because where provision is made, and care is given, it is always an attraction."

This was, of course, only natural. Welfare services and improved living conditions obviously attract more people, which, in turn, make

Average population density per square mile: Megalopolis

it more difficult to improve their lot. During famines in India, it has been observed, not only peasants but also sacred cows stream into the cities. They expect more help and care in these better-organized societies.

New York and other Megalopolitan cities thus attract more than their share of underprivileged people from the South and from Puerto Rico, much as a hundred years ago they attracted "the wretched refuse of [Europe's] teeming shore."

But then or today, the migrant is not lured only by the prospect of charity—though this may motivate Indian cows. The lure of the city is rooted in the reasonable expectation of fair economic and cultural opportunity.

Urban slums may be dismal. But they hold greater promise of a good job and a good school for the children than rural slums.

Because there is crowding in the city, there is also a more organized society. Its organization adjusts resources to needs. It provides a variety of specialized occupations.

### The city offers constantly more varied and better jobs.

Technological progress has, of course, succeeded in reducing the relative number of human hands needed in agricultural, mining and some manufacturing production. But the number of people required to service the total process of economic production is still increasing. This trend is not new. Since 1870 there has been less relative growth in manufacturing employment but a steady increase in the complex of the white collar occupations and in jobs in maintenance, trade and transportation.

At the same time manufacturing is becoming a less important component in the city economy. For a number of reasons plants and factories, as we shall see, are leaving the big cities. Thus servicing, clerical and professional work, and the new specialties and trades these create, are becoming the truly urban occupations.

In the constant changing and churning within Megalopolis the "office industry" is now beginning to dominate downtown. It offers more and more specialized, better-paid jobs and good working conditions.

# Suburbanization

The changing and churning within modern cities is also causing them to spill over into the countryside.

There are two basic reasons for the continuing urban sprawl. One is the increasing dispersal of manufacturing and warehousing. The other is that, with the automobile and mass transportation, office and professional workers can now live farther away from their jobs.

They can move into green suburbia.

The hub of heavy industry in the United States is no longer in Megalopolis. It has been moving westward since about 1870—across the Appalachians to the triangle formed by Pittsburgh, Cleveland and Chicago. Specialized manufacturing scattered all over the Middle West and even to the Pacific Coast. Textile plants began to migrate toward the cotton fields and the cheap labor of the South.

This trend continues. Yet certain industries still remain or locate in Megalopolis. Clothing and printing industries, for instance, need to be close to their enormous consumer market. The advanced electronics industry is dependent on Megalopolis' large pool of especially skilled workers.

But even these industries migrate within Megalopolis. Many leave the city because they find either their workers or their locations, or both, too expensive. Often they need more space for expansion.

They build modern plants in small towns or out in the country. But they stay, of course, within easy reach of good transportation. Thus the influx of manufacturing has been greater between the main cities, along the axial roads and railroads, than in outlying districts. Some

**Our city population changes . . .**

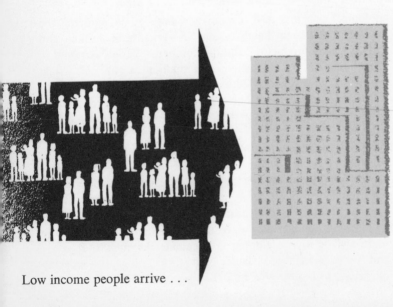

Low income people arrive . . .

middle-income people leave

industries, however, particularly those near Philadelphia, prefer tide-water access.

The extent of this movement is hard to measure. Industrial and commercial land use has never been as carefully studied as housing.

But we do know that certain manufacturing specialties concentrate in certain areas; that space for expansion is important to any viable industrial enterprise; and that the recent trend in industrial buildings has been to spread horizontally rather than to rise vertically.

Since low, rambling one- or two-story buildings require more land, and acreage is cheaper outside the city, this trend has further accelerated sprawl. And since plants depend on transportation, this movement, too, has been along the main axial belt of Megalopolis.

### Offices, banks, department stores, hotels

and even hospital buildings, however, have been built in the opposite way. In contrast to industrial plants they have tended to shoot up vertically into high-rise towers. One reason is, of course, that these offices need to be close to one another and in or near the central business district where land is expensive. (Another reason is the real or fancied prestige of a skyscraper which towers above all others, especially the buildings of one's competitors.)

At the same time a greater separation in space has developed between the production and the nonproduction facilities of firms and entire industries. Factories and warehouses are now miles, even hundreds of miles, away from administrative offices and research laboratories. While the offices concentrate in the city, the laboratories are beginning to crowd the suburban periphery.

The result of all this is that a pattern of land use is evolving for metropolitan space. There is a kind of division of labor by which

. . . and, at the same time, so does the suburban population

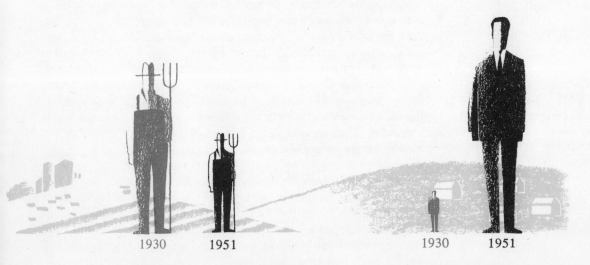

1930    1951                              1930    1951

The farm population declines and . . .        the rural non-farm population increases

different locations are the site for specific activity. Thus form and function of land use are becoming increasingly inseparable.

### Residential suburbanization

may be less obvious. Seen from the air, wooded residential areas seem more thinly populated than they are. And official statistics do not always fully account for all the people who live in one community and work in another.

Those suburbanites who make their living in the city have responded to the lure of less crowded country living. Wealthy people have long considered country houses and the recreation they offer a symbol of status.

The villas of rich merchants have dotted the landscape around Florence since the Renaissance. In the eighteenth century manorial homes were built not only outside the great European cities but also around Boston, New York and Philadephia. Some of them were merely summer residences. But others were occupied most of the year and their owners commuted to their city occupations.

Growing affluence, better education and shorter working hours, not to mention the automobile and the increasingly dense network of highways, have now made suburban living possible for vast numbers.

Plants grow horizontally

### The automobile contributed

to suburban sprawl, which accelerated as more cars and highways became available in the 1950's. According to the 1960 Census, the biggest population increases took place on the suburban periphery of the main population centers. Farther away from the main highways and large employment centers, urbanization proceeded less intensely and mainly along roads and around ponds and creeks.

Residences, obviously, do not scatter alone. Commercial establishments, both wholesale and retail, follow their customers to suburbia. And the jobs they offer, in turn, attract more residences. Here, too, scatteration is considerably helped by the automobile, which makes trade and light industry independent of railroads and waterways.

The statistics do not, however, properly reflect what is happening to the landscape. The density of population is measured in administrative subdivisions and people are counted where they live, not where they work. Thus an area dense with smokestacks may appear on the map as empty of population while a wooded part of suburbia may show up as urbanized because it is dense with people.

The nebulous character of suburbanization is, of course, not unique to Megalopolis. Similar sprawl is evident in many parts of the country, particularly along the Pacific Coast from San Francisco to Los Angeles. California's densities, however, seem worse than they are. Buildings stand out boldly in the barren landscape. Megalopolis still has far more buildings and people.

But they are shielded by trees.

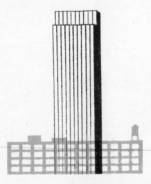

Offices grow vertically

# Are Cities Obsolete?

Why do people and factories move? Is there really no space for them in the old cities?

We have mentioned the romantic, though at times illusionary, lure of greenery and fresh air. Many offices move onto farm and forest land because their workers live there and because it is less expensive for them to expand there.

Others move to the suburbs because their competitors or related businesses are already there.

But most frequent is the notion that the city core is obsolete. This notion is largely subjective.

Whether a home, factory or office is obsolete depends on how much money the owner has to improve it, how well the occupant likes it, and how easily it can be replaced with a more profitable or more fashionable one.

### Obsolescence in a building in an affluent society

is as much a matter of fashion as of economics. The cost of rehabilitating old houses does not, for instance, discourage a great many people from wanting to live in Washington's Georgetown or Manhattan's Sutton Place or, for that matter, in remote and romantic old barns. But these are isolated instances where the relatively wealthy defend charm and convenient downtown location against blight. Elsewhere deterioration is a vicious circle. When city neighborhoods become socially obsolete because of their location, maintenance and upkeep expenses are cut. They promptly become physically obsolete as well. And they turn into slums.

But the problem of obsolescence in buildings cannot be reduced to the problem of slums. Slums are the result and not the cause of it. It is untimely deterioration, then, which must be attacked. For whether it spurs blight or renewal, obsolescence accelerates the displacement of people, activities and entire neighborhoods. And this, in turn, eats up the land and accounts for sprawl.

According to the statistics, the condition of housing in Megalopolis is surprisingly good. Only California has a higher ratio of dwellings in good condition—with running hot and cold water, private toilets and baths—that are not overcrowded. What overcrowding there is, in terms of persons per room, is largely confined to Negro neighborhoods because white people often are unwilling to let Negroes settle where they would like and could afford to.

Trapped between the slums and the glassy new apartment towers of Megalopolis, furthermore, are a growing number of middle-income families with small children. They are *forced* to move far out into suburbia because the cities no longer offer them adequate housing at reasonable cost. This gives rise to the question, as recently put by one planner, whether the city is condemned to be a place only for "the rich, the lame, the halt and the blind, the poor, the aged and the minority group."

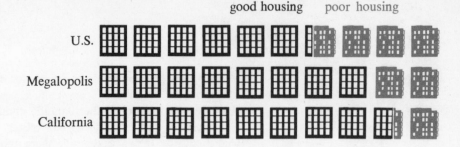

good housing · poor housing

U.S.

Megalopolis

California

**Housing in Megalopolis is better than the national average . . .**

### Lack of upkeep of old buildings

is, of course, the most important cause of obsolescence. But this is not because the structure has worn out but because of its use by successive waves of occupants. In most cities old houses have "come down" from their well-to-do original owners. They have sheltered family after family of newcomers, each one poorer than the family before. The immigrants from abroad recently gave way to in-migrants from the South or from Puerto Rico.

Most families are willing to take care of their homes. But they often do not own them. And some landlords squeeze as much profit as possible from the buildings before such structures are ripe for slum clearance and a tidy cash payment for the land.

The demand for technical conveniences—as well as gadgets—is a further factor in obsolescence which has nothing to do with the actual soundness of a building. Such things as air conditioning and fast elevators are no longer considered luxuries but necessities. And these demands have, in the past twenty years, modified the entire design of houses, apartments and especially office buildings. As in cars, Americans want the latest model even if it is only a slight or seeming improvement over the old one.

### Zoning, taxation and credit

affect obsolescence of buildings as well as age and social and technological change.

Zoning goes back to building limitations for fire protection in Boston in 1692 and an ordinance of 1706 that banished powder mills from the vicinity of the city's residences. The first comprehensive zoning regulation in the United States was enacted in New York City in 1916. Today zoning regulates almost all urban areas in the country.

Zoning should, but rarely does, express the community's intent, wisdom and resourcefulness in protecting the future as well as the present. The idea of zoning is primarily to protect land values and assure stability in built-up areas. But in the way in which it has been used zoning does not control urban decay. On the contrary, by petrifying urban improvement it also speeds the deterioration of buildings. If zoning, for instance, prevents an owner from converting his large, highly taxed, and once elegant but now empty townhouse into a number of small apartments, he is more or less forced to let his white elephant deteriorate.

The process is further accelerated by our system of taxation on the basis of assessed value of land and buildings. The value of the land may increase. The value of physical improvements, on the other hand, depreciates with age and use and thereby increases the cost of public services.

Taxation should encourage proper maintenance and upkeep of buildings to prevent decay and make major operations less necessary. Yet the present system does the opposite. It punishes an owner for making improvements by raising his tax assessment. It rewards him for negligence by reducing his taxes on less valuable property.

Credit for building improvement is subject to similar thinking. Once a city neighborhood is suspected by the bankers to be on the way down, it is almost impossible to get improvement loans. Again, this speeds up obsolescence, not just of individual buildings but of entire neighborhoods.

### Federal policies

have until recently tended to slow down the renewal of buildings and cities. Federal mortgage insurance was most readily available to middle-income people and for detached suburban homes. While this may not have caused urban sprawl, it certainly facilitated it. And it worked against renewing old city neighborhoods and city centers.

With the Housing Act of 1949 which authorizes Federal aid for urban development and redevelopment the fight against decay was at least begun. During the 1950's Megalopolis has used this means of attracting privately financed redevelopment more extensively than any other section of the country. As yet the effect of the program has been minor, particularly in terms of desperately needed new low-cost housing.

### Basic to all these factors

which conspire to speed obsolescence—original construction, new demands for technical improvements, zoning, taxation and credit—is the mobility of the American people. One out of every five Americans moves every year. Or, looked at in a different way, the whole nation is resettled every five years. If Americans really wanted to stay where they live and work, they would find the means of maintaining, modernizing, and equipping their buildings. And they would protect the social standing of their neighborhoods. But to many of us, moving seems an easier solution than costly repairs and so a whole neighborhood goes down.

This is a matter of immense importance, not only to land use and urban planning, but also to the entire national economy. A boon to the construction industry and to real estate speculation, rapid deterioration of buildings is increasingly expensive for the rest of us. We pay for it in urban renewal, in highway construction and other means of transportation, and in the damaging cost of urban sprawl and the erosion of human values.

**. . . and not unduly crowded**

West

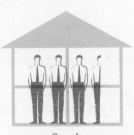

South

Megalopolis

# 4  THE REVOLUTION IN LAND USE

The explosion of the city beyond its limits brought about drastic social and economic changes that happened faster than they were recognized.

The old contrast between town and country has given way to a new distinction between entire regions that are urban and entire regions that are agricultural. The most obvious and advanced urban region in the United States is Megalopolis. The largest and most typical agricultural region is the grain-growing Great Plains.

This does not mean that there are no towns in agricultural regions or no farming in urbanized areas.

Obviously numerous towns and cities in agricultural regions have developed trade and industry. Their main purpose, however, is to serve the surrounding farm economy. Farmers in an urbanized area, on the other hand, may produce as much of certain farm goods as those in an agricultural region. The difference is that they are part of a new, essentially urban, economic and social organization.

This organization is both cause and result of new patterns of land use—the symbiosis, or close "living together," of what was previously classified as urban and rural.

The old pattern was determined by the simple "push off the land" and "pull of the cities." Farm work, thanks to machinery and chemicals, needed fewer workers. And these workers were attracted by new jobs in the city.

In Megalopolis this push-pull force is still at work, attracting farm people to the city. But it has been complicated by a simultaneous counter-pull of manufacturers, trade and new residents to suburbia and rural areas. This accounts for the constant churning both within and beyond officially designated urban areas.

**It is difficult to measure this process.**

Up to 1950 the Bureau of the Census classified all people living within defined urban territories as urban and all those living beyond them as rural. In 1950 the Census redefined urban population to include the inhabitants of densely settled urban-fringe areas and of unincorporated places of 2,500 or more outside the urban fringe. With this revision the number of places classified as urban by the U. S. Census increased from 3,464 in 1940 to 6,014 in 1960. The percentage of urban in the total population rose from 56.5 percent in 1940 to 70 percent in 1960.

This definition comes closer to accounting for the actual situation but it still does not fully describe it. It counts everyone as rural who is not classified as urban. And most of us associate a rural population with people who live off the land. The fact is, of course, that most of them now derive their income from urban pursuits or commute to city jobs.

■ Water  ⬡ Woodland  ■ Housing  ⬭ Pasture  ⬭ Cropland

The statistics of the distribution of the "rural nonfarm population" —that is, people who live in so-called rural areas but are not engaged in farming—therefore provide a somewhat better understanding of what is happening. The size of this group varies from county to county. But for almost all the rural territory in Megalopolis it was greater than 70 per cent. The figures also show that this group moves about more frequently than either the urban group or the rural farm population, reflecting suburban growth.

Suburbs have often been described as "dense settlements," and this in turn is taken to mean that the city in the conventional sense is spreading. Woodland, however, still makes up nearly half of the Megalopolitan area.

In 1950 practically every county of Megalopolis, outside of the cities themselves, was more than 12 percent wooded. In New England the proportion of woodland reached more than 60 percent. And in other counties not situated along the main urban axis from New York to Baltimore it remained more than 30 percent.

This means then that the growing and mobile "rural non-farm population" lives in housing predominantly amidst wood and brush. It is a population which obviously does not deplete woodland but, on the contrary, pushes the farmland out and pulls the forests in. And increase of woodland, due to the spread of suburbia, can be observed in almost every large region of the United States east of the Mississippi as well as in Europe.

The new pattern of land use cut by urban sprawl thus does more than increase the population density of previously rural areas. It also, paradoxically, increases woodland and, as we shall see, the output of a number of farm products.

Agriculture occupies more space than do cities and suburbs and therefore still dominates the landscape in large parts of Megalopolis.

47

# Agriculture in Megalopolis

But farms are the main source of sites for new housing, industry and highways and are therefore constantly dwindling.

Yet, in terms of output per acre, Megalopolis is one of the foremost agricultural areas in the United States. It is matched only by the fertile irrigated valleys of the Pacific states and the leading fruit- and vegetable-growing areas. This productivity is still vigorously expanding. Paradoxically, the most efficient and prosperous farms are those about to be liquidated by the city. Farm productivity in urbanized New Jersey, Rhode Island and Connecticut leads that of all other states in the Union.

Nor are farmers economically threatened. Those who sell usually get enough money for their land to retire comfortably for the rest of their days. Those who stay in farming have a greater share in growing markets.

The threat, rather, is to the city. For, as existing open spaces between the metropolitan complexes disappear, the present problems of congestion, communication and outdoor recreation are further compounded.

**Farmers cultivate the market rather than the land**

in Megalopolis. They no longer conform to the old image of the rugged individualist who tills his land and tends his herd.

Megalopolitan farming is characterized by a sophistication found in no other part of the country. Most everything grown here could be grown elsewhere, often on better soil at less cost. And for some products the competition is severe.

But Megalopolitan farming has an asset that few other areas can match: the greatest number of customers with the highest income. To take advantage of this asset Megalopolitan farmers must be smart managers who specialize in high-value crops and perishables for direct human consumption.

The land value per acre of Megalopolitan farms is higher than farm land anywhere else in the country, but this value is due to location rather than to fertility. Farm property on the seashore of Martha's Vineyard, for instance, which until recently was despised and neglected, now fetches fabulous prices—sand, beach peas, poison ivy and all. The crop it raises is serenity, a rare and valuable commodity in Megalopolis.

Another characteristic of Magalopolitan agriculture is the high degree of tenant farming. This does not appear in the Census statistics. For what happens is that while farm estate owners live on their property, they have it worked by tenants. The Census considers a man a tenant only if he rents the entire property.

A good many Megalopolitan farmers are dairymen and poultrymen who are essentially manufacturers. They buy low-cost raw material in the form of feed grain and sell high-priced products such as meat or milk. It is more advantageous for them to bring in cheap feed from across the Appalachians than to raise it themselves on their small and not particularly fertile farms.

Others concentrate on crops that cater to the special tastes of city people, such as mushrooms, or that might spoil if they had to be brought in from afar, such as flowers and garden plants.

Such farming needs business judgment, skill, special equipment, considerable capital and good long-term sales contacts to assure steady supplies and sales. It takes advantage of two developments in farming since 1920: the progress in plant and animal breeding and the replacement of the horse by the machine. Progress in techniques has, for instance, significantly increased the production of milk per cow. Eliminating the draft horse has also done away with the need for large pastures, oats and hay.

Yet the work of the Megalopolitan farmer is in no way less noble or more artificial than that of his colleague in the Great Plains. In fact, he produces fewer surpluses and thus costs the taxpayer less in subsidies. But he, too, benefits from all the devices of easy profits that American farm legislation affords.

## Dairy farming is especially well organized.

Dairying requires the greatest amount of land and is therefore concentrated on the western fringe of Megalopolis, outside the main axis of urban expansion. While relatively cheap, this land—in the Piedmont and the Limestone valleys—is also among the most fertile in the region.

Milk production also requires the greatest amount of capital. It is mostly in the hands of large private firms whose profitable business is protected by government. Local authorities watch out for the consumer, while the Federal government protects the interests of the farmer.

A boon to both is the organization of so-called "milksheds." These are areas designated by city and sometimes state governments as the only ones which may supply milk (and often cream) to the consumers under their jurisdiction. The production, processing and transportation of this milk must meet legal health requirements established by the consuming city or state. Inspectors assure compliance.

This protects the consumer but it also assures a steady market for the dairyman. The price of milk sold in the city is fixed. Thanks to Federal supports it is high enough to pay the producer well. Pound for pound the Megalopolitan dairyman receives almost twice as much as dairymen in Wisconsin or Minnesota, the heart of America's dairy land.

But while the bulk of midwestern production goes into butter and cheese, Megalopolis puts most of its milk and cream into bottles. By various ingenious methods Megalopolitan farmers manage to produce more and more milk on less and less land. Their business is vulnerable only insofar as they become increasingly dependent on the Corn Belt's control of the feed supply.

With a large and stable demand and an abundance of capital, it is not surprising that a number of dairy farms provide a comfortable

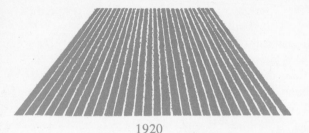

1920          1960

Decrease of farm land in Megalopolis

gentleman-farmer living for many. In New Jersey a company furnishes "cow-sitters" for gentlemen farmers who wish to get away from their stables. Some of them also engage in raising horses or fattening beef cattle, a somewhat more expensive pursuit than dairying.

### Estate farms

exist all over the United States, and they are particularly plentiful— although now also diminishing—in Megalopolis. Most of them are owned by people who derive their main income in the city and maintain their estate, with its Angus cattle and neat white fences, for pleasure or as a place to retire after years of commercial or political responsibility.

The great advantage of such estates for the rest of us is that they help form an attractive and vitally necessary green belt around the big cities. But high taxes make it increasingly difficult to keep land simply because it is beautiful. In general, only owners of small estates with a simple residence can afford the luxury of a field of goldenrod and daisies.

### Poultry farming has been revolutionized

during the past thirty years. Before 1930 most farms had a flock of laying hens as a sideline and all our chicken and egg supply came from these flocks. Today poultry farming, especially in Megalopolis, is a highly specialized and scientific business.

Raising one pound of broiler now requires only three pounds of feed rather than the four it used to take. And it takes less time (and thus less labor and overhead) to raise a bird for market.

Since poultry are now fed entirely on concentrated feed, they require very little land space. This is why poultry farming is independent of the quality of the soil and is now found on costly real estate close to big cities.

The production of broilers, in contrast to eggs, is more highly regionalized. The heaviest concentration is on the Delmarva Peninsula where the winters are mild (saving shelter and heating) and where long tradition has developed the greatest skill.

Many people with city jobs and farm homes still keep chickens as a hobby. But only large-scale operations which have a high capital investment in labor-saving automatic machinery and which buy feed

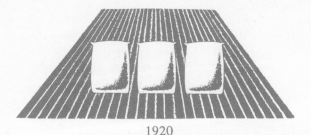
1920

1960

Increase in food produced in Megalopolis

in great bulk are really profitable. Even poultry farms whose yearly sales are $25,000 or more sometimes lose money in the close squeeze between the market value of poultry and operating cost.

Amateur and semi-professional poultrymen are nevertheless numerous enough in Megalopolis to keep competitive pressure on the commercial farms. The greater threat, however, comes from states outside Megalopolis. Competition is possible because eggs are not as perishable as milk. Broilers can be kept by freezing. And poultrymen have no milksheds to protect them.

Georgia, with its cheaper labor, is increasingly turning from cotton to poultry raising. California, Iowa and Minnesota are already top egg producers. And Federal soil bank subsidies are an added incentive to mid-western farmers to convert surplus feed grains into more valuable livestock products. They turn back their fields to forestry or wildlife and convert their barns and sheds into poultry houses. As they draw government subsidies for not working in the fields, they can easily undersell Megalopolitan poultrymen.

The famous ducks of Long Island are typical of specialty farming in Megalopolis. The duck farms along the southern shore of Long Island supply mainly nearby New York restaurants and food shops whose many Chinese and Central European customers have retained their traditional fondness for fat duck. But many of these farmers are now selling their land to summer vacationers and commuters.

## Cash crops and specialized farms

usually require relatively little land but a high degree of skill and considerable hand labor. Much of Megalopolis' farm labor is seasonally employed and recruited from southern states, the West Indies and from among university students during their summer recess.

Fruits, tobacco, nursery stock, greenhouse products, white potatoes and other vegetables are the primary products of Megalopolitan cash crop farmers.

In cash crops, like poultry raising, the amateurs tend to drop out of the game and the professionals tend to go in for large-scale operations. This does not necessarily mean increased acreage but the use of better equipment and more highly skilled labor. Only about 4,000 acres of muck soils in Orange County, New York, for instance, produce the fourth largest crop of dry onions in the United States.

New Jersey and Delaware devote a greater proportion of their cash crop acreage to vegetables than any other state. New York and New Jersey similarly lead in the space used for growing flowers under glass. Among the country's top twenty counties in the production of nursery and greenhouse specialties, ten are in Megalopolis.

It is sometimes by luck or accident that a farmer discovers some specialty that enables him to hold on to his farm in the face of rising taxes and increasingly tempting offers from suburban developers. A farmer in Connecticut, for instance, discovered that he can profitably combine dairying with raising Christmas trees. His cows keep the grass low between his rows of 100,000 trees and thus reduce the danger of fire. College boys help him cut the trees at Christmas time.

Not all farms are specialized, of course. In southeastern Pennsylvania, particularly in fertile Lancaster County, are many and surprisingly profitable general-purpose farms, stocked with a fine dairy herd, a feed lot for beef cattle, a pen of hogs, a large flock of poultry, and, in addition, plots of tobacco, hay and grain. The whole family and/or hired farms hands pitch in.

But the "Old MacDonald" type farm is dying out. The majority of commercial farms are streamlined and specialized enterprises. Thus there are gardeners who raise exotic vegetables exclusively for Chinese restaurants. There are others who produce sod for suburban lawns or game birds for gourmets.

The center of mushroom production in the United States is southeastern Pennsylvania. It is within overnight shipping distance of all large cities of Megalopolis. And such geographic location is a matter of careful calculation.

Some of the commercial farm executives are just as likely to be in New York or St. Louis as in their offices on the farm. And they are flown back and forth in company planes by company pilots.

**Size of farms and farm value**

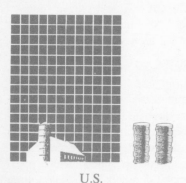

U.S.

**Urban encroachment on farm land**

is not yet as serious a threat as it may seem—*to the farmers*. As we have seen, they compensate for the loss of their land by making greater investment in labor and equipment. They turn from common field crops that are fed to livestock to commodities than man consumes directly. Farming in Megalopolis is increasingly becoming a factory culture. Agricultural operations are being as compactly housed as people and maintained in the same way, with feed brought in from cheaper land.

Thus considerable land still remains. In southern New England and southeastern New Jersey, Delaware and Maryland, for instance, wood and brush still grows on many farms. This is due only in part to rocky soil. The more important reason is that the farmers don't need the land to grow feed.

Megalopolitan farmers have, in fact, learned to count on steadily increasing land values due to urban pressure. One Connecticut dairyman remarked: "We farmers raise three crops. We go onto a place in our youth to raise a family. We spend our working years producing milk. When we are ready to retire we harvest enough capital gain from the land to keep us in our old age."

The fact that an unproductive woodlot in Essex County, Massachusetts, is worth more than an acre of the best limestone hayland in southern Virginia bears him out.

Farmers who want to stay in business take their land profits, move on to poorer soil and bring it into production. This is happening throughout Megalopolis. Long Island and New Jersey potato growers have gone to Delaware where land is cheaper. By investing more money for drainage and fertilizer they harvest as many potatoes as before. Former Rhode Island dairymen who sold their valuable land now sell as much milk as ever in Massachusetts.

### In the long run

this matter cannot be left entirely to chance and individual initiative. Agriculture can be maintained only if we distribute the land more wisely than now. As matters stand, urbanization takes over the best soil with the highest capacity for production.

One possible solution is agricultural zoning which protects not only the farmland but also its owner against rising taxation. First developed in California, such zoning is now applied in Manheim Township, Lancaster County, Pennsylvania, one of the finest natural agricultural counties in the world.

This solution, however, does not seem to appeal to most farmers. The "poor farmer" doesn't mind grieving the loss of his land as he lolls in Miami Beach while the "rich city slicker" works the rest of his life to pay for it.

Only in a very few counties are soil scientists employed to help plan the use of land according to soil types and terrain conditions. Such specialists have aided farmers for years. But they are rarely called in to plan the proper urbanization of land. This is surprising since it is more expensive to construct buildings than to plant alfalfa.

Intelligent land planning could avoid the leapfrogging sprawl which outflanks some farms while it overruns others. This destroys the rural community without establishing an urban one. Suburban grey zones result, as ugly and inefficient as any in the city.

Such suburban grey zones are perpetuated by investors who quickly move in and buy the remaining farms without developing them. They let them go to seed and erosion, knowing that the increase in land value is greater than the interest they have to pay on the money they borrowed. They also prefer to pay the capital gain taxes on their speculation rather than the steeper taxes on income earned as interest or dividends.

Such unused land may profit the speculator but it is most expensive to the community—and not only in aesthetic terms. Such land can no longer be considered for the orderly planning of floodwater impoundments, roads, sewers, schools and other vital facilities. New housing that is actually built is pushed farther and farther away from the city. This means longer and more expensive sewers, more utilities and roads, and greater transportation problems.

New means and policies for the proper use and distribution of land are urgently needed.

**Size of farms and farm value**

Megalopolis

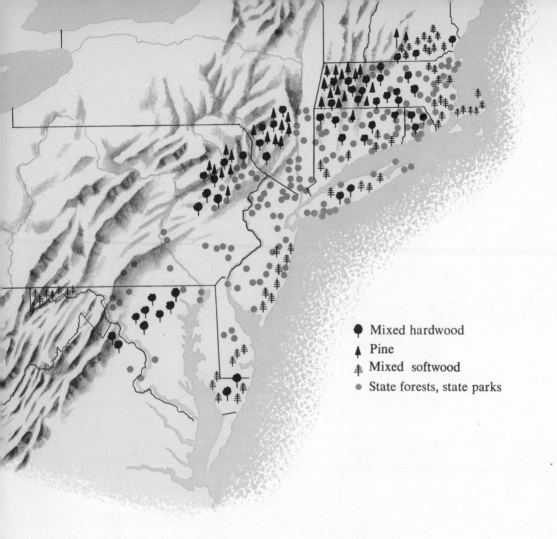

● Mixed hardwood
▲ Pine
‡ Mixed softwood
● State forests, state parks

# Woodland and Wildlife

Woodland, surprisingly, still covers half of Megalopolis—16.2 million acres. Even more surprising, since 1946 forests are again increasing.

True, a closer look reveals that dense suburban housing is often found under the trees. They are a prerequisite of the American dream house which perches behind a front lawn in the center of a miniature feudal estate, no matter how ridiculously small.

But even excluding the resulting park-like suburbs, there are plenty of woods in Megalopolis. This is typical of the forested part of the United States east of the Great Plains. And it seems that the spread of cities and the resulting retreat of agriculture favor the increase of woodland, though its quality has deteriorated.

The reason for the increase is that land abandoned by farmers and speculatively held in the wake of suburban development is often allowed to re-forest. It is a good way to let the investment grow without use of expensive labor. And there are the possible dividends of grazing, hunting, timber cutting and Uncle Sam's Soil Bank.

City people, furthermore, seem more concerned than farmers about preserving woods which they desire for recreation and water supply.

We are, however, not concerned enough, considering that 16 million acres of woodland and a population of 37 million figures out to less than half an acre per person. It seems hardly adequate.

Wooded green belts around our urbanized areas are essential to the public welfare and not only because they help conserve fertile soil, water supply and wildlife. We also believe, at least since Thoreau and Emerson, in the health-giving and spirit-restoring "goodness" of nature.

## Man's actions have deeply affected the forests

over the years. When the European settlers arrived, all of Megalopolis was clad with deep forests in which the Indians burned clearings to facilitate travel and attract game.

By 1825 half of the land in the Northeast had been cleared to secure farmland and timber and firewood. There was a short reprieve as better farmland was pioneered in the West and new forests took over abandoned fields and pastures. But from 1830 on, the steam sawmills invaded the forests, claiming the old stands for lumber and the second growth for charcoal and other uses. Since industry preferred softwoods, a hardwood invasion developed and the sawmills moved farther south. By 1910 the northern stands had grown back, only to be depleted again in a few decades. Now there are not enough softwoods available and new waves of cutting must take more hardwood.

Recently, "commercially selective" lumbering is being applied. It takes the valuable species and leaves the less desirable trees standing. This further speeds the transformation of Megalopolitan forests into a valueless coppice of hardwoods. The resulting abundance of brush-stage woods, in turn, has also favored the present overpopulation of deer. Deer eat young seedlings and happen to like the commercially more valuable ones best.

A further threat are forest fires. The danger is greatest in dry seasons, of course, and in pine forests. But the threat comes mostly from man—only 4 per cent of forest fires are caused by lightning or other natural causes. City people cause fires through ignorance and carelessness. Farmers use fire as a tool—to prepare top soil for the regeneration of pines, for instance—which gets out of hand.

As a result of all this the U. S. Forest Service found in 1950 that our forests are understocked in desirable timber trees. This is especially true around large cities. But the woods all over Megalopolis are full of sawmills which cannot meet the demand for good timber close to their market.

## Most woodland is privately owned.

There are no federal forests in Megalopolis. State and county forests, too, have only recently been established. The conservation movement has been far more successful in the West and South. Nor is there much ownership by the forestry industry, aside from the 8 per cent it holds of the Massachusetts woodland.

Most woodland holdings are small and belong to active or abandoned farms. Half of the commercial forest land in heavily wooded states are no larger than 100 acres and less than a tenth are bigger than 500 acres.

Many of the owners have inherited their woodlots and hang on to them as an investment even though they live in the city. Few of the lots belong to farms. And a good many that belonged to large estates now have become golf and country clubs or public recreation areas.

### Recreational parks,

an ancient privilege of the rich and mighty, have been provided for the people of Megalopolis only since the early decades of this century. Originally this curtailed crowding. But now that practically everyone has a car, a taste for the great outdoors and a portable transistor radio, nature's solitude is moving farther and farther away.

The invasion of vacationing hikers, hunters or fishermen is causing owners to close off their woodlands, so that the growing number of city people finds less and less open space.

It is true that nowhere else are there as many state parks exclusively devoted to recreation as in Megalopolis. Long Island alone has thirteen. Jones Beach State Park is nationally famous and Heckscher State Park, farther away from New York, is rapidly becoming so. Most of these parks are "functional." That is, they are designed for swimming, picnicking, camping, hiking and skiing, and sometimes feature hotels, cabins and boat basins.

But they are also overcrowded (Jones Beach has some 200,000 visitors on a clear summer day) and small. And there are far from enough of them, particularly around Philadelphia and Baltimore.

### Hunters fare better than hikers.

Although the number of hunters in Megalopolis has almost doubled since 1938, they all find plenty of game close to their city homes or —at any rate—within less than a mile's walk from their automobiles.

This is astounding in view of the fact that earlier generations of Americans had just about wiped out deer, grouse and wild turkey. Early in the century several Megalopolitan states had to prohibit deer hunting or at least doe shooting altogether and brought new stock from the West to refuge areas.

These deer have proliferated to such an extent that there now is,

1900          1950

Lumber production by states 1900-1950

New York        New Jersey        Massachusetts        Connecticut        Maryland        Pennsylvania

as already mentioned, an overabundance. Urban hunters help protect them in a way, not only by their adherence to preservation prac-
tices, but also because they rarely take the time or energy to penetrate the woods very deeply.

The danger of the sport is, however, almost greater for the hunter
than for the deer. Posting against hunting by annoyed landowners
forces the hunters into public areas. These then are no longer safe
because of crowding. Sport clubs often rent hunting privileges from
landowners, and well-stocked commercial preserves are available for
those who can pay the admission. But neither diminishes the growing
need for more public grounds.

Publicly owned land is also needed to maintain and increase game,
because it has proven as difficult to persuade private owners of good
game management as of good forestry methods.

### The task of preserving wildlife,

a federal responsibility for migratory game and a state responsibility
for resident animals, is increasingly difficult. Modern "clean" farming,
with its excessive use of poisonous chemicals, disturbs the balance of
nature. There are, for instance, not enough insects to support many
game birds. Poor cover and poor feeding have drastically cut down
the number of the popular bobwhite quail. The decrease in cultivation in Megalopolis depletes the food supply of other wild game.
Wild turkeys and the heath hen are practically extinct. In addition to
deer, only the ruffed grouse, once almost gone, skunks, raccoons and
rabbits seem to have staged a comeback.

The task is to protect what wildlife remains and to introduce new
species. One solution is artificial stocking. It has worked fairly well
for pheasants and to a lesser degree for bobwhite and wild turkeys.
But since only a disappointing number of these birds survive preda-
tors and an unfavorable environment, they are now released from
state game farms only a short time before the hunters come to shoot
them. This is a costly proposition—about two dollars a pheasant in
Connecticut—and to many people a somewhat depressing one.

Equally sad is the disappearance of migratory waterfowl. The wetlands where brants, canvasbacks, redheads and scaups, white-winged
scoters, Canada geese, coots, widgeons, pintails, blue-winged teal and
other waterfowl and shorebirds live and rest along their Atlantic Fly-
way from Labrador to the Antilles and South America, are shrinking.
The creation of new bird refuges does not keep pace with the pollu-

Delaware
       Virginia
       Vermont
       New Hampshire
       Maine
       Rhode Island

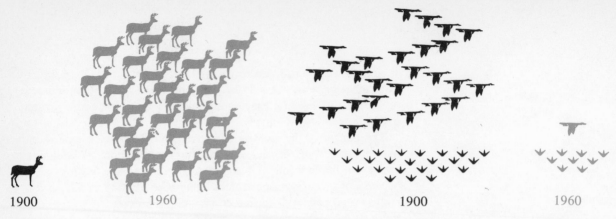

1900        1960                   1900           1960

Deer have vastly increased in Megalopolis . . .        . . . but wetland and water fowl are decreasing

tion (for mosquito control or cranberry management) or filling (for building, highways or rubbish dumps) of remaining wetlands.

But here, too, the U. S. Fish and Wildlife Service and the seaboard states are now at work. Both buy up marshes and ponds, and improve and stock them for the sake of both the birds and their hunters.

### Fishing has also vastly increased

in Megalopolis, although not as sharply as in the rest of the country. Megalopolitan fishermen can also fish in or along the sea, which requires no license. Fishermen, just like hunters, are bedeviled by posting, and the government's efforts to persuade landowners to open their land to the sport are of little avail. Here, too, public land acquisition is the most effective solution.

Fishermen would like to see city water reservoirs opened up for their sport. But this is not considered safe unless the water is filtered. The American Water Works Association frowns on fishing and boating in reservoirs even then. Nevertheless, the State of New York and some reservoirs elsewhere permit their reservoirs to double as recreation areas, apparently without untoward consequences.

### Fish, too, have been drastically affected by man.

For one thing, dams, deforestation and industrialization have warmed up the rivers to the point where many cold-water species, such as trout, have declined or disappeared. Pollution, due to industry, has the same effect as it depletes fish food and reduces the oxygen content of the water.

Moreover, dams hamper the migratory species. The shad is the only migrant which has, with the help of man's fish elevators, managed to survive in Megalopolis. It is now holding its own in a number of rivers, including the Hudson and Connecticut.

But man is also stocking some waters, particularly with trout. Not that the trout survive any better than game birds. Fingerlings die and river improvement seems too expensive. Fish hatcheries now release fully grown trout, but only to be caught—as 80 per cent of them are.

So while fishing and hunting are increasing, they have become largely an artificial affair.

1900       1960            1900       1960

More people hunt . . .           . . . and take out fishing licenses

### Preservation and increase of woodland

is not only a need which contributes to recreation and the decor of living. Although we don't know all there is to know about the interrelation of forest and water, it is obvious that good forest management is needed to assure the water supply and prevent floods. Megalopolis has a growing thirst for water as well as serious flood problems. We do know that woods are needed to let the water filter down and stabilize underground aquifers, or water-bearing rock or sand beds. And they prevent water from running off slopes.

Better forest management could also help produce more timber than is now produced without conflicting with a better water policy or recreation. Well-planned recreation areas would not require much land. Even if they were significantly multiplied, they would occupy only a small fraction of the woodland now available.

The difficulty in restoring our forests for proper industrial use is the expense and time it takes. Private landowners, most of whom want money out of their land and are afraid of taxation, are therefore little inclined to undertake the job. The system of taxing property on the basis of assessed value does not encourage sound forest management.

To date improvement of privately owned forests has been attempted by regulation and incentives. Regulations with their fixed rules, which often do not apply to a given situation, have worked poorly.

Incentives, such as free seedlings or soil bank subsidies, also have their drawbacks. Good forestry needs continued efforts. Incentives must therefore be followed up with "compulsory advice" from well-trained professionals. And such management must be coordinated with hunting policies. It might be well to help develop game animals other than deer, such as pheasants, which provide good shooting but do not damage seedlings.

Megalopolis requires increased efforts of large staffs of experts, a whole industry of big farms and hatcheries, constant land acquisition, and a good deal of research to maintain the precarious balance of nature. Urban hunters and fisherman who object to government management of open spaces might do well to remember that it is the government which provides the game and fish for them.

59

# Uses of the Land

Megalopolis is becoming so densely urbanized that some people are driven to dire forebodings. Soon, they fear, there will not be enough land left to raise food for our needs and to live on.

The fear of running out of food seems unjustified. As in all advanced Western countries, food production has grown much faster than food consumption, despite the population increase.

The fear that we may be running out of space is justified only if we think of open spaces in terms of the wilderness which awaited the pioneers. Traditionally we have thought of America as the land which provides everyone with ample choice as to where to live, how to live, what to do for recreation and where to work. This freedom of choice is part of the stuff the American dream is made of.

But the dream is changing. Wide open spaces still exist, even in Megalopolis. But what good is the ample, increasingly wooded land in the Appalachian foothills or in northeastern Massachusetts to a New Yorker or Washingtonian? He cannot find work there. Nor can he commute a hundred or two hundred miles to a desk or workbench in the city.

Because of such considerations, people in recent years have settled along the main highways, and for less. They came prepared to be somewhat fenced in and to accept satisfactions and opportunities other than those the old frontier offered. Today their suburban dwellings manage to combine easy access to work, recreation and good schools with fresh air and a rosebush by the door.

This compromise involves longer commuting and devours more land. But people pay the price for a greater sense of freedom than the same amount of floor space in a city apartment would offer.

Manufacturing, too, puts easy access first on the list of things to consider when selecting a new location. The means of transporting goods are often far more important to the manufacturer than the means of housing his employees. A sudden influx of new residents can frequently cause discomforts to the old ones. It also creates new problems for local government. And traffic jams. In most of Megalopolis industrial migration is, however, still easily absorbed.

Even the wilderness, or at least ample space for the enjoyment of the great outdoors, still exists. When we complain about its disappearance, we usually mean open space within our reach.

### "Running out of space,"

then, actually means "running out of easy access to desired places." Access is no longer a matter of distance measured in miles. It is a matter of organization and arrangement in terms of time, comfort and cost involved in transportation. The dispersal of people and manufacturing—and thus the urbanization of Megalopolis—is the result of automobiles and highways and the affluence to pay for them in such abundance.

As noted earlier, the land occupied by urban, or so-called "special," uses actually occupies only 20 per cent of the total area of Megalopolis. The problem is not really that of running out of space. It is that the excessive demand for transportation keeps outrunning our ability to provide good highways or good mass transportation. As a result an increasingly greater part of what ought to be leisure time is spent on getting about.

And despite the intense interpenetration of urban and rural, Megalopolis continues to build up its congested central cities. Its horizontal sprawl is accompanied, and perhaps complemented, by a vertical rise in the old urban cores. The skylines of Manhattan, Philadelphia, Boston, and many of the smaller cities such as Newark and New Haven, are changing more rapidly than ever.

Many people who work in these skyscrapers live in suburbia. This accounts for the fact that, in terms of population increase, the suburban rings grew just about six times faster in the 1950's than the central cities. Yet only part of this growth is due to city residents moving to suburbs. Most of the new suburbanites come from outside the metropolitan area, although we don't know just how many and whence they came.

### Change will continue

The revolution in land use is bound to continue. Megalopolis has reshaped its environment more than once and will not stop at this stage. The present emphasis on urban renewal is one symptom of this constant change.

Suburban sprawl is expensive, not only because of the large amount of land it devours, but also in terms of what the suburban family must spend for transportation and services.

The metropolitan explosion has, on the other hand, contributed a great deal to the national wealth. Residential structures alone, exclusive of the land, are estimated to make up a quarter of that wealth. Our extravagant land use has added additional wealth in terms of other construction as well as the consumption of automobiles, gasoline, lawn mowers, do-it-yourself tools and innumerable other items. The amounts are beyond estimate.

In general, the families who choose the suburban way of life can afford these expenditures, although it may leave them with little to spend for other things or for savings.

Even today, only 20% of the total land area of Megalopolis is urbanized

# New Trends

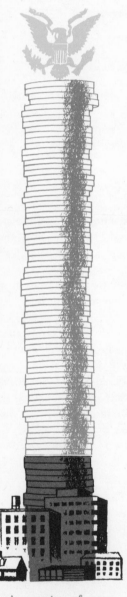

A quarter of our
national wealth
consists of residential
structures

In making their choice between "spacious living" and "easy access" a great majority of these middle-income people have so far chosen space. (Low-income groups, of course, never quite had the choice since they cannot afford to commute. And the very rich often live in elegant apartment towers near their offices and spend their weekends spaciously in the country.)

There is, however, no reason to assume that middle-income people will continue to make the same decision. While the construction rate in Megalopolitan cities has continued to increase in recent years, it has levelled off in the outer suburbs.

This is logical, as these suburbs are concentrated along the chain of adjacent metropolitan areas where land values and construction costs are constantly rising.

### The rising cost of suburbia

influences more and more people to make their choice in favor of "easy access." The trend is towards living closer together—in townhouses and apartments—and closer to town.

It is also increasingly doubtful that the high rate of capital accumulation and redistribution actually balances the high cost of residential sprawl. The wealth suburbia is adding must be paid for in ever rising taxes for increasingly expensive highways, schools, sewers and utilities.

Nor have suburban yards in any way decreased the need for recreational land or, for that matter, for playgrounds and sport facilities for youngsters. We are therefore now searching for less expensive ways to solve the problems of a growing population.

One of them is the housing of people in high-rise apartment buildings in the city or close to the city core. The Swiss-born French architect Le Corbusier has advocated such apartment towers since the 1920's. They can be spaced far enough apart to leave light, air and recreation space. And on the ground between them, lively neighborhood centers with shops, restaurants and places of entertainment and recreation could be built in a pleasant and inspiring setting to relieve the tedium now associated with this kind of building.

Another solution to accommodate urban growth without excessive sprawl is the rehabilitation of aging buildings and neighborhoods. This is now an important part of federally assisted urban renewal activities. We are beginning to recognize the need for urban conservation and are developing better and less expensive ways of bringing deteriorated buildings up to modern standards.

Most important, our communities are becoming aware of the enormous cost of letting city neighborhoods decay.

Half a century ago we began to conserve our forests and other natural resources. It is high time that we begin to conserve our urban resources. They are not unlimited.

# 5  EARNING A LIVING INTENSELY

The livelihood and great economic power of Megalopolis rest on its industry and commerce. Yet these take up very little space.

The richest fifth of the American population—the population of Megalopolis—earns its living on less than one thousandth of the country's land.

As we have seen, historically the people of Megalopolis launched their prosperity and importance in the world with their foreign commerce. Today the majority of workers hold commercial and financial jobs or work in administrative and research activities related to manufacturing. Direct employment in manufacturing amounts to only one quarter of the total.

Yet it was the manufacturing plants which attracted people to Megalopolis in such large numbers and which swelled the cities.

The fact that factories now tend to move out of the area to less crowded parts of the country and that Megalopolis' share in American manufacturing has been steadily dropping is therefore causing some concern.

Will Megalopolis lose vital jobs for its people?

This will not necessarily happen. Future employment opportunities, so vital for the area's continued momentum, seem to depend less and less on manufacturing. The modern economic evolution, sparked by technological advances, points, rather, to a decisive increase in commercial and white-collar occupations.

But both manufacturing and commerce depend on Megalopolis' continued function as the nation's economic hinge. And this, in turn, raises the important problem of transportation and communication within the area and between it and the lands across the Appalachians and across the ocean.

The hinge function, as we have seen, has in the past relied on an exceptionally intricate network of roads, railroads and inland waterways as well as on the sea lanes. In an era of airplanes, pipelines, telephone, radio and television these seem to lose their historic significance. Traffic conditions within Megalopolis are, furthermore, sadly worsening.

This is especially true in the "downtown" area where administrative and white-collar activities must concentrate in order to grow and thus to provide the necessary job opportunities.

But along with its traffic problems the "downtown" center of the city is threatened by physical and social decay. If this is allowed to continue, the migration and decentralization of the office industry will follow that of manufacturing. And with it will go the jobs.

The pretty green suburbs could not long survive unemployment in the central city. The people who live there would naturally have to pack up and migrate to new places of employment.

To date Megalopolis has frequently found it profitable to waste its space and material resources. But it would be disastrous were it to waste its human resources as well.

# Manufacturing is Changing

Though direct employment in manufacturing provides only one quarter of all available jobs in Megalopolis, it remains the most important of all the major employment categories. It keeps the economy going.

Megalopolis, as we noted, has lost plants to other parts of the country and is no longer the leading production center of the nation. But the decrease in manufacturing is only relative.

In absolute terms, in numbers of people employed and in value of goods produced, manufacturing is still most important in Megalopolis, though it may not be growing as fast as elsewhere.

In 1958 Megalopolitan factories employed more people than Italy and Sweden put together. And they turned out greater value than both these countries plus the United Kingdom. Only the industrial Middle West—the triangle defined by Chicago, Pittsburgh and Buffalo—can boast a comparable concentration or perhaps an even greater one. (Exact comparison is difficult because Megalopolis and the Midwest specialize in entirely different products.)

### Accessibility

is the secret of this impressive record. Cost of supply and delivery loom large on every manufacturer's balance sheet.

Consider, for instance, the advantages of location in the midst of Megalopolis' massive consumer market. This is particularly important for food industries whose products will spoil rapidly; for apparel which is subject to rapid changes in fashion; for electrical and

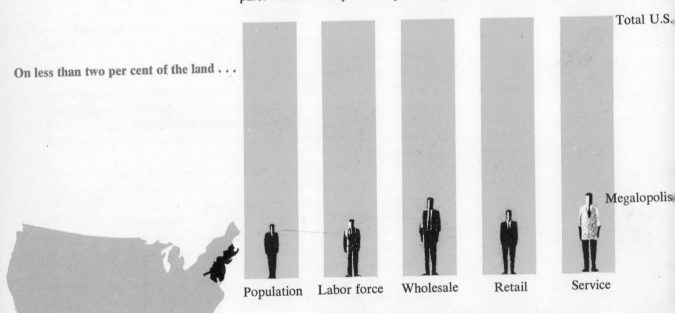

On less than two per cent of the land . . .

Total U.S.

Megalopolis

Population    Labor force    Wholesale    Retail    Service

. . . Megalopolis does nearly a third of the nation's business

64

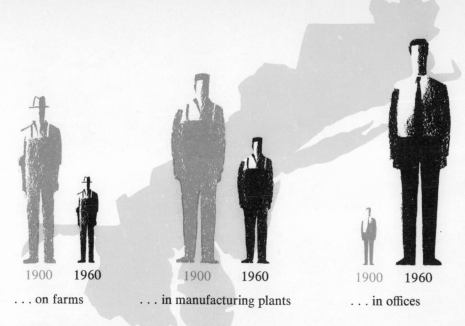

1900    1960         1900    1960         1900    1960

. . . on farms        . . . in manufacturing plants        . . . in offices

A growing percentage of Americans earn their living with office jobs

electronic products which need careful handling; for printing houses which must maintain close personal contact with their customers; and, of course, for construction industries. For all of these and others it is almost essential to be on the spot. And all industries which depend on face-to-face contact thrive in Megalopolis.

Another factor which favors Megalopolis is power supply. When coal was the major source of power, location on or near coalfields naturally saved the great cost of transporting this bulky material. In the nineteenth century the eastern Pennsylvania coalfields thus contributed greatly to the industrialization of Megalopolis.

But Megalopolis managed to keep up with a changing technology. It secured both adequate and cheap power from other sources. In the beginning there were fuel wood and charcoal from the woodlands, waterfalls on local streams, and local coal deposits. When these sources became insufficient other sources of energy were brought in from afar.

Petroleum is now imported from many parts of the world. Natural gas comes from Texas, Louisiana and elsewhere. Hydroelectric power is fed in from the regions to the north and west. And soon electricity from nuclear power promises to become available.

Another important factor in the concentration of industry is that one plant always seems to follow others, at least until a point of saturation is reached. Industry attracts industry for two reasons. First, industries often depend on one another as suppliers and customers. Secondly, industrial towns and neighborhoods already have a labor market for the newcomer to draw on.

**Megalopolis produces just about everything . . .**

. . . from airplanes to zippers. The New York metropolitan region alone boasts 420 of the 450 industries named in a recent Census listing. And it is safe to assume that the remaining thirty categories can be found elsewhere in Megalopolis. While there are, for instance,

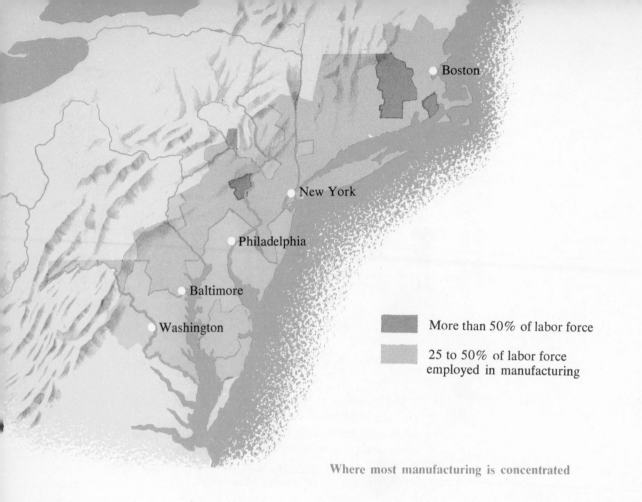

Boston

New York

Philadelphia

Baltimore

Washington

More than 50% of labor force

25 to 50% of labor force
employed in manufacturing

Where most manufacturing is concentrated

no large steel mills around New York City, one need go no farther
for them than eastern Pennsylvania or the suburbs of Baltimore.

The emphasis, however, is on "lighter" products. Megalopolis tends
to specialize in the finishing stages of manufacturing and in producing more complicated and delicate kinds of products for mass consumption. The area leads the nation in the concentration of men's and
women's clothing, millinery, drugs and medicines, footwear, house-
hold furniture and electrical machinery.

This trend, like others, started in New England. It partly explains
why manufacturing value and employment have continued to grow
even though the number of large plants has decreased. But it does
not explain why some kinds of manufacturing have moved out of the
area while others remained. It would seem that all categories would
react similarly to such factors as the impact of crowding and the
proximity of the consumer market.

### Variety in itself brings vitality

to Megalopolitan manufacturing. Because of its high wages the area
is under constant competitive pressure from other parts of the country.
These pressures force flexibility and inventiveness. To keep their
wheels spinning and workers employed, manufacturers constantly in-
vent a better mousetrap, a new fashion or a novel gadget.

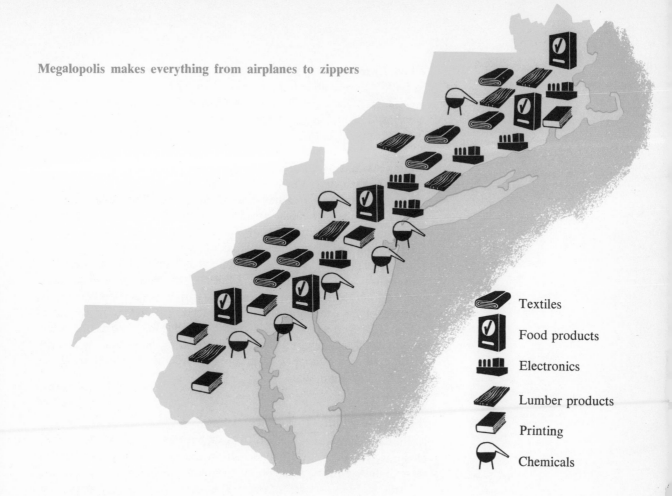

Megalopolis makes everything from airplanes to zippers

Textiles
Food products
Electronics
Lumber products
Printing
Chemicals

More important is the fact that like other areas, but somewhat faster, perhaps, Megalopolitan manufacturing is increasingly changing its character. It specializes in the upper and final stages of refining products as well as in management research and development. Research, the "incubator" or "nursery" phase of industry, then spawns new industries making new products. These new industries may be located anywhere in the country.

Ordinary manufacturing—the mass production of standardized goods—still goes on of course. But its importance for megalopolis is declining. The region owes its high employment and prosperity largely to the kinds of manufacturing which cannot easily replace human skill and labor with machines.

There are other reasons for the relative stability of Megalopolitan industry.

### The primary metals industry,

for instance, though it started 200 years ago along the seaboard, grew mainly west of the Appalachians. Since World War II, however, such plants have come back to Megalopolis.

The reason is that an increasingly larger share of our needs of iron ore, copper and bauxite is supplied by imports from abroad. The higher grades of iron ore accessible to open-pit mining close to the

Great Lakes became exhausted. But they are abundantly available in Latin America and on the west coast of Africa.

Imports of iron ore now account for over 20 percent of our national consumption and have increased about thirty times since 1937. It is therefore logical that new steel plants have been built on the shores of Megalopolis in the heart of large steel-consuming and scrap-generating markets.

Another reason is that the high cost of mining and transportation have made the re-use of metal scrap profitable. This pays when the supply of discarded metal objects is plentiful and steady. It is not surprising that densely populated and affluent Megalopolis meets this qualification best of any area in the country.

Metal scrap, furthermore, is supplied not only by individuals discarding old cars and refrigerators but also by industry. This is called "prompt industrial scrap generation"—an important factor in the Megalopolitan economy. Connecticut leads the nation in the rapid turnover of iron and steel, followed by Michigan, Massachusetts and New York. Megalopolis as a whole is ahead of the rest of the country in the recovery of copper. It accounts for about a quarter of all industrial scrap aluminum.

### How industry attracts industry

is illustrated by metal scrap. Manufacturing plants using metals obviously depend on primary metal industries. But they also furnish these industries with scrap, both from their own left-overs and the discards their customers furnish. This cycle proved very important during World War II and the Korean War when metal shortages developed.

The chemical and petroleum industries follow the same general pattern as the primary metals and for the same reasons. Their raw material—crude oil—is brought in by sea, and their "on-the-spot" market is enormous. The most impressive concentration of oil-refining plants is along the lower Delaware. But there are others around the great Megalopolitan port cities as well.

In general it can be said that the heavier industries tend to concentrate west and the lighter industries east of the Hudson.

### Manufacturing clusters away from the big cities.

The great concentrations of industrial workers are in southern New England (but not near Boston), in eastern Pennsylvania (but some distance from Philadelphia), and in some New Jersey counties (but quite far from both New York and Philadelphia).

The reason is, of course, that the large cities offer their inhabitants more lucrative job opportunities while smaller cities and towns are usually unable to attract other kinds of economic activity.

Industrial concentration, however, is still greatest along the axial belt of Megalopolis. In the past manufacturers preferred to settle between two large markets and close to their workers. They thus helped to fill the spaces between the original urban nuclei, often

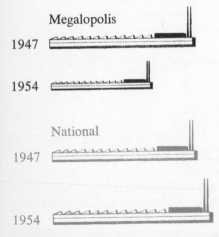

Large plants decrease

Megalopolis

1947

1954

National

1947

1954

Textile

1947

1954

Electrical Machinery

1947

1954

Megalopolitan industries change

turning relatively distant, outlying neighborhoods—sometimes called "exurbia"—into a more dingy "suburbia."

In the past twenty years, however, since practically all workers have cars and adequate roads are available, industry has tended to move away from the old clusters. Plants can now draw their workers from as far as twenty to fifty miles away.

Generally workers moved to suburbia before the factories did. The reason, of course, is that workers seek to escape from city congestion and deterioration. And they can do so more easily than factories, which constitute a considerably greater investment than residences and don't become obsolete as quickly.

But the reverse is also true. Obsolescence has driven manufacturing plants out of the city but workers have been unable or unwilling to follow.

New and large plants are at times built far away from housing for the employees and with little prospect of new housing developments within reasonable distance. This is because communities welcome plants since they add to the tax base, but restrict new housing for low-income workers since that housing must be serviced with schools, water, sewers, etc. This forces the workers to commute long distances and clutters the highways. Developers sometimes spot such situations and build new residential clusters. And suburbia keeps sprawling.

### There is still enough space

and suburbanization is still easy. If a manufacturer is not satisfied with the location of his plant in downtown Boston he can easily find a site in the suburbs or in the next county. If another wants to leave Connecticut it is not too much trouble to move to New Jersey or eastern Pennsylvania.

Manufacturers are apt to prefer such short moves to a long one, say, to Texas. They stay on familiar ground and continue to take advantage of Megalopolis' high concentration.

In a word, this advantage is "mass"—mass of people, money, consumption, transportation, labor, and even mass of junk, as illustrated by the importance of scrap metal.

Manufacturing nevertheless tends to move southward within Megalopolis. This is more often than not the result of expansion rather than displacement. But this same centrifugal force is beginning to take industry out of Megalopolis altogether.

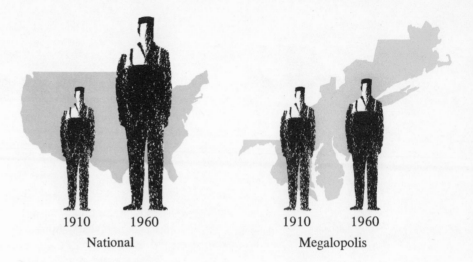

1910    1960          1910    1960
National              Megalopolis

**Manufacturing jobs in the nation as a whole increase faster than in Megalopolis**

Some plants, notably textiles, have moved to the southeastern states. Modern transportation and local accessibility are no longer as important to them as cheap, abundant and unorganized labor, relatively inexpensive real estate and tax advantages.

Despite this loss in manufacturing plants, which is greater than that of some other sections of the country, the number of people employed in manufacturing continues to grow. The increase, however, is much slower than that for the nation as a whole. In the first half of this century manufacturing employment in Megalopolis rose only 10 per cent compared to a national increase of 60 per cent.

To some extent this slow growth in manufacturing jobs is due to automation. Machines do the job of people, and with the help of such machines each individual worker produces far more than he used to. This is borne out by the fact that not only production has increased, but also the dollar value of the goods produced.

It is, nevertheless, also true that in Megalopolis the axiom that industry attracts industry is no longer always true. Some areas and urban cores seem to have reached industrial saturation. This is particularly evident in parts of New England and in the outskirts of New York City.

It is safe to assume that many new industries would like to locate in Megalopolis if the area were less crowded and its labor and taxes less expensive.

But what probably holds existing industries and, despite crowding, still adds a reasonable number of new ones is Megalopolis' vast pool of labor. Nowhere else can one find such a variety of workers. They range from poorly skilled and low-paid newcomers from Puerto Rico and the South to highly skilled and highly paid craftsmen. While competent personnel is even more important in white-collar activities, it is also becoming increasingly important in manufacturing. What used to be a blue-collar job may soon require a degree in engineering.

# Commercial Organization

Industry in Megalopolis is closely linked to the region's unique commercial organization.

The people employed in wholesale and retail trade and in different services as well as the owner-merchants of unincorporated businesses comprise almost a third of the total Megalopolitan labor force.

This sizable organization distributes the products of manufacturing not only within Megalopolis itself but sometimes all over the world. It also provides the incentive for the development of new products and industries.

Commercial organization includes more than merely trade. It also involves a number of services that take care of the necessary operations of *transfer*—transporation and communication, corporate and business legal counsel, accounting, advertising, real estate, banking, brokerage, insurance and other financial transactions.

As products and commerce become more complex, so does transfer. A greater variety and specialization of professional services is needed. And their cost becomes an increasingly sizable factor.

### Retail trade and selected services

naturally follow their customers. But in the days when consumers were thinly spread across the vast expanse of the United States, retailing was even then relatively concentrated in the areas of higher population density and income. These were, of course, mainly in the Megalopolitan cities.

The generation before ours could find the greatest variety of merchandise only in New York, Boston, Philadelphia, and other large cities. While people seldom had to go far to buy food, they would travel considerable distances for their furniture or expensive fashion goods.

All this has changed radically in the past twenty years. The great prosperity of the 1950's lifted the American standard of living to undreamed-of heights. Food consumption became rather uniform throughout the country. The average American family owned its own home, and furnished it with a rapidly increasing number of mechanical gadgets.

To meet these new needs shopping areas developed in nearly every town. They are stocked with a greater quantity and variety of merchandise than ever before.

True, there are also more people who can afford special foods and more expensive furniture and luxury goods. Those wealthier customers and many city residents still shop in the great stores in the big cities. But they represent only a small fraction of retail business. On the whole, the share of big cities in the national total of sales has decreased. This tendency is accelerated by the stores themselves. They follow the customer by establishing branches as near his doorstep as possible.

71

## Shopping Centers

have created new market places or small "downtowns" within the apparently unorganized, nebulous structure of America's metropolitan regions. Almost all settlements have at least one.

The reason is, of course, that the scattering of residences has caused an inevitable scattering of retail trade and services. The speed of this diffusion varies. Supermarkets are usually first in new suburban developments, with personal and repair services never far behind.

Like the old medieval markets or "fairs," shopping centers are usually located at important crossroads where they are equally accessible to town and country. And some of them, again like some of the old "fairs" beyond the town walls, form the core of new business districts.

The large shopping centers, just like the downtown business districts, do not confine themselves to retail stores alone. They also include banks, service stations, post office branches, barber shops and beauty salons, and sometimes even a movie theater. They strive to attract social life and occasionally succeed in becoming real community centers.

There is no doubt that the suburban shopping center has made a definite imprint on the American way of life. Some people feel, however, that the rapid mushrooming of shopping centers has excessively scattered the suburban consumer market. It has certainly taken a great deal of business away from the old urban cores.

In a way this is, perhaps, all to the good. The new competition has forced improvements downtown. In recent years downtown merchants in a good many cities have banded together to meet the common threat by revitalizing Main Street, providing better parking, and in other ways making their area more pleasant to visit and shop in.

Formerly the main shopping area of a town or city was centered in the main business district—the place where other important commercial operations were carried on. Downtown, where the main roads or transit lines converged, was the city's great market place.

New York City's large department stores were the first to branch out and decentralize. They invaded the suburbs in the wake of the great consumer exodus. They have been forced to do so because in the past ten years their downtown business dropped to about half of what their suburban stores earned.

The variety offered in suburban stores is, of course, far less enticing than what is offered by the downtown stores with their more numerous and diversified customers. On the other hand, in many kinds of merchandise, suburban department store branches often compete with small specialized stores which cluster around them in shopping centers.

## Selective service trades

also scatter, but far less rapidly. Some of these services still cluster in the heart of the city. Most of them serve entertainment and hotels and local residents as well as the wealthy at the national and international crossroads where businessmen and visitors from all over the world come together.

Increase in retail trade in New York City and in its suburbs

The great cities thus retain a number of functions which shopping centers or even satellite "downtowns" can't take away from them. People are too thinly spread in the suburbs to justify duplication of all the services and attractions the city can offer. They are, furthermore, a fairly sophisticated lot, particularly in Megalopolis, and used to commuting. A good many of them don't mind making a trip downtown for specialized shopping or a visit to their favorite beauty parlor, optician or dentist.

### Wholesale trade

employs fewer people than either retailing or the selected service trades. It consists of larger establishments with a wider system of commercial relationships. The extent of wholesale trading usually determines the commercial significance of a crossroads. It creates more transportation, more white-collar jobs and more credit management. It often also attracts banking and manufacturing.

The seaports of Megalopolis have been the great wholesale markets of America ever since the end of the seventeenth century. They are a natural function of the "economic hinge."

In the eighteenth century Boston and Philadelphia vied for first rank in wholesaling. Then, at the close of the War of 1812, the British dumped huge bulks of goods on the wharves of New York. These were the exports they had gathered to send to the United States once normal relations were again resumed. The New York merchants rose to the occasion. They turned New York into the largest wholesale market of the nation, the main hub of its foreign trade. This attracted the stock exchanges, and later the insurance and advertising industries and the theaters that have made New York what it is.

Cities                                          Suburbia

Wholesale trade remains largely in the city

New York City's leadership as a wholesale market became, by
1939, even more marked than its leadership in retailing. And from
this time on the main axis of Megalopolis appears on the map of the
United States as a continuous chain of substantial wholesale centers.
Nowhere else is there a comparable grouping.

Some of these centers are highly specialized and serve the entire
country. Among them are the fur and diamond markets of Manhattan, in which relatively few people handle relatively small quantities of goods of considerable value. New York City and one or two
other cities also handle wholesale trade in fancy foods and delicacies,
imported wines and liquor, and similar luxury items.

Wholesale houses for ordinary foods, distributed in large quantities
to large numbers of people, are usually located near a large market.
They cluster in big cities where both sellers and buyers can take
advantage of diverse services from entertainment to legal advice.
New York, for instance, became a leading wholesale center in part because of its reputation of lavishly entertaining merchants.

Yet wholesaling is also spreading out within the main metropolitan
areas. Bulk merchandise requires large warehouses which are easily
accessible by truck. The crowded streets of congested business districts do not offer this easy access. Parking space is lacking unless special facilities are provided and this is costly on expensive city land.

Wholesale trade nevertheless tends to stay as close as possible to
the large cities. In both New York and Philadelphia food wholesale
markets have been moved from old congested inner cores—but only
from lower Manhattan to the Bronx and from downtown Philadelphia
across the state line to New Jersey.

Decentralization, furthermore, does not involve all phases of the
wholesale trade. Only operations requiring large warehouses move to
the periphery. The business offices often are downtown. It is safe to
predict that before long no wholesale goods will be brought into the
city that are not to be consumed or processed there. But trading and
price bargaining will take place in the city as this can be done with
samples. The market, in other words, as a place where business is
transacted will remain concentrated. Warehouses, however, will continue to be scattered on the city fringe and in the suburbs.

Where very large quantities are involved, wholesale trade must, of
course, continue to rely on shipping. It also depends on close contact
with financial institutions. And it will continue to be located in places
inviting to merchants. These factors alone would seem to assure that
wholesale trade will remain an important part of the powerful commercial organization of Megalopolitan cities.

# Maritime Commerce

The maritime commerce of Megalopolis is concentrated in Boston, the Port of New York, the Delaware River ports, and Baltimore.

By the end of the nineteenth century, as the country became economically more self-sufficient, it seemed that maritime commerce would decline in importance. By the middle of the twentieth century, however, the tide had turned once more in favor of seaports, particularly those of Megalopolis. They now handle 40 per cent of the nation's sea trade.

Four developments helped in this revival of shipping: The growing need for oil from the fields of Texas and Louisiana; the opening, in 1914, of the Panama Canal, which facilitated shipping to and from the West Coast and the entire Pacific; the intense overseas shipping during and after the two World Wars; and the increase in imports, mainly from countries bordering the Atlantic.

According to long-standing international usage, seaports are ranked according to the volume of their trade with foreign countries. In assessing the role and problems of maritime traffic in Megalopolis, domestic coastwise shipping is, however, of almost equal significance.

## Coastwise shipping

consists mostly of raw material cargoes from Gulf and West Coast ports. It involves large ships, a great variety of important goods and a long ocean voyage.

The tankers carrying petroleum and petroleum products make up the major part of this traffic. They deliver their oil from the fields of Texas, Louisiana and, sometimes, California not only to the large Megalopolitan cities but also to smaller ports such as New Haven, Bridgeport, Norwalk and Stamford.

Coal is another important coastwise shipping cargo, although it has been somewhat on the decline. But ores, especially iron ore and bauxite, are gaining importance among dry cargoes everywhere and are increasingly shipped to Megalopolitan ports.

In terms of international trade, the Delaware ports rank above New York as they handle a larger amount of foreign tonnage. But if coastwise trade is included, New York is well in the lead. It handles 13 per cent of the nation's total combined foreign and domestic shipping.

Taken together, again combining foreign and domestic trade, Megalopolitan ports lead the rest of the nation in ship movements and merchandise handled, except for outbound shipment.

The fact that incoming shipments exceed outgoing ones at a ratio of about four to one is not surprising. For the imports, as we have seen, consist largely of raw materials arriving on the Delaware River and in Baltimore.

The outgoing shipments, on the other hand, consist mainly of expensive finished products. In terms of the value of shipments, therefore, ingoing and outgoing are almost balanced.

## Megalopolis' share of the
## nation's shipping

Number of vessels visiting ports

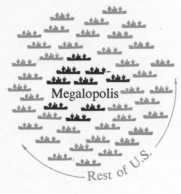

Megalopolis

Rest of U.S.

Tonnage handled

Megalopolis    Rest of U.S.

Import cargo

Megalopolis    Rest of U.S.

Export cargo

Megalopolis    Rest of U.S.

## Megalopolitan ports have more diversified commerce

than any others in the nation. Their ships, sailing both under American and foreign flags, ply regular routes which neatly envelop the globe. This permits specialization in small cargoes which may not fill the entire ship but which require speedy delivery. Manufacturers find this "maritime express" highly desirable. They often go out of their way to ship via New York, Philadelphia and Baltimore because they can rely on regular schedules calling at many ports. There is little costly warehousing and delay.

Shipment of manufactured goods—notably machinery and electrical equipment—is bound to increase as the demand for them rises in underdeveloped countries. Bulk trade, however, can and must be decentralized to avoid overloading the great ports. The trend, therefore, is much the same as in wholesale trading. The more expensive kind of merchandise remain concentrated in the old centers while the less expensive kinds will continue to scatter.

## Port operations do not employ many people.

It takes relatively few hands to perform each operation in the life of the port. But it takes highly skilled labor to pilot and berth a vessel, load and unload goods and passengers, dredge the channels, and furnish the ship's services and supplies.

All of this, taken together, makes a big port a large-scale industry and a substantial source of revenue.

The flow of passengers and goods naturally requires inland transportation by truck, rail, inland waterways and air. There must be warehouses and offices for traffic management, freight forwarding and brokerage, insurance, and industries which build, repair and service both ships and docks.

In short, an efficient harbor requires a whole world of specialties. And just as industry attracts industry, commerce attracts commerce. This is exemplified by the liners operating from New York. The first regularly scheduled line, the "Black Ball Line," was inaugurated in 1816. Now there are 160 lines calling at the Port of New York.

## Shipping, too, is undergoing change.

Harbors are expanding to avoid congestion. And ship traffic is moving, though unwillingly, away from the main hubs. The New York harbor, for instance, now stretches to the opposite shore of New Jersey and to Port Newark, though both are administered by the New York Port Authority.

This expansion is necessary, for New York seems to be consolidating into the main Atlantic gate of the United States for general cargo and particularly for passengers.

New England's maritime activity, on the other hand, is slackening somewhat. There are complaints that the port of Boston may be "drying up." It shows a decrease in liner calls and cargo traffic. The reasons given are mainly the difficult access to Boston by land (there are only a few bridges across the Hudson), the keen competition from New York, and Boston's somewhat obsolete facilities.

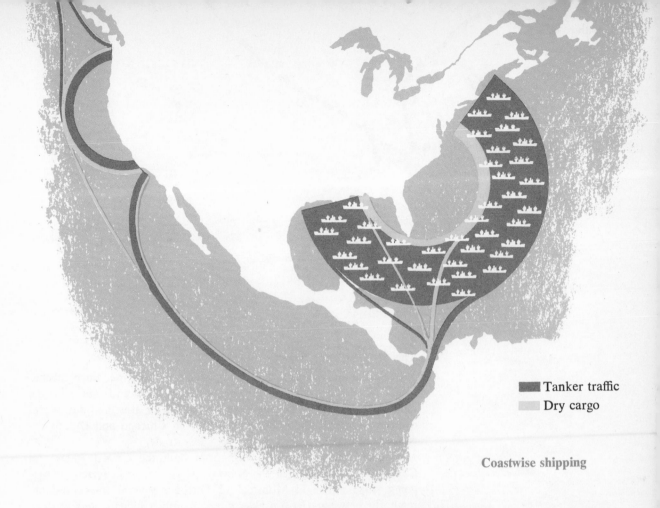

Tanker traffic
Dry cargo

Coastwise shipping

The Delaware River ports with their steadily increasing shipments of petroleum and ores are still growing. And so is Baltimore, although less rapidly than before the 1950's.

Each of these major ports likes to consider all of the United States and, in winter, a good chunk of Canada as its hinterland. This concept is, of course, somewhat naive. Each of the four great seaports, located within one hundred and two hundred miles of each other, cannot possibly have a fixed commercial realm of its own. Nor could such thinking account for their traditional lead in the nation's maritime trade, stuck away as they are in a small corner of the country.

It was, in fact, the flexibility of the Megalopolitan ports—an ability to rapidly change clients, merchandise and destination—that fostered their phenomenal growth.

The fact is, as we have suggested, that each of the four ports tends to specialize somewhat. This specialization leads to some cooperation. A ship from abroad which unloads in one of the ports and does not find sufficient return cargo there can complete the load in another. While 160 lines come into New York, about 110 regularly call at Philadelphia.

The four Megalopolitan ports, in other words, share not only the same oceans but also the same hinterland and the same economic fortunes.

They also share the same competition with other port groups on the Atlantic and Gulf Coasts and, since 1959, the St. Lawrence Seaway.

77

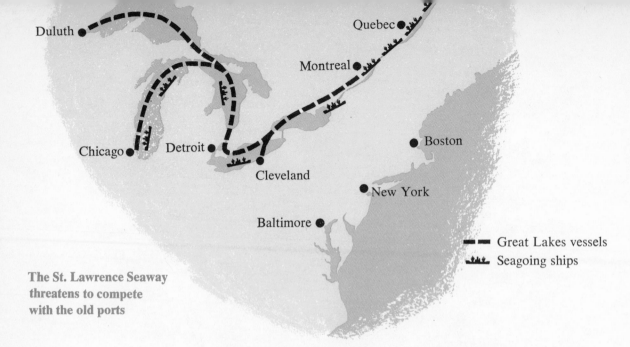

Duluth

Quebec

Montreal

Chicago    Detroit

Boston

Cleveland

New York

Baltimore

■ ■ ■ Great Lakes vessels
🚢🚢 Seagoing ships

The St. Lawrence Seaway
threatens to compete
with the old ports

### The St. Lawrence Seaway

may eventually threaten a very important part of the hinge mechanism. Now the ports of the northeastern seaboard are still the natural intermediary between the Great Lakes area and the world overseas. Once Buffalo, Cleveland, Detroit, Chicago and Duluth become seaports Megalopolis may well lose trade.

Already much outbound grain from both the United States and Canada is going through the Seaway. It is then transferred to seagoing ships either in Montreal or Quebec. Several lines now ply regularly between Great Lakes ports, mainly Chicago, and western European ports. They may soon keep regular schedules, even when the Seaway is frozen, by terminating at an ice-free port—a possibility that raises hopes in Boston.

By the time the Seaway reaches its scheduled capacity of 50 million tons in 1968 it may divert as much as 10 per cent of the cargo from New York, mostly grain. Other Megalopolitan ports are worried, too.

But while the Seaway will undoubtedly boost the Great Lakes region, its threat to Megalopolis is still remote. The gravitational pull of its huge well-organized market is formidable, indeed.

### Air travel and air freight

are expanding rapidly, both here and abroad. Air freight will, of course, hardly surpass seaborne trade in volume but it is likely to increase considerably as larger jet planes are built.

In this field, too, the hinge function of Megalopolis is evident. So much national and international business is transacted here that Megalopolitan airports, especially those of New York, have become an obvious pivot in the domestic and overseas networks of the airlines. The axial belt of Megalopolis is also one of the greatest arteries of air traffic in our time.

Growth will here again inevitably lead to decentralization. New York remains the hub of air transportation, but other cities are now developing their airports in an attempt to keep pace with an ever rising demand.

# The Money Market

Traditionally the term "money market" means the exchange of national currencies. But this is nowadays only a minor part of modern finance. We use the term here to include all the varied and complex activities involved in the handling of money and credit.

The money market is the business of "the financial community." These people work not only in the Wall Street area of Manhattan but also in the new skyscrapers along Park, Madison and Fifth Avenue and in other Megalopolitan cities. They are bankers, brokers and insurance agents, as well as corporation lawyers, financial executives of large corporations, chamber-of-commerce officers, foundation officials, and even professors and journalists who specialize in economics and finance. And they maintain close connections with manufacturers, government officials (including representatives of foreign governments) and advertisers.

### The financial community

is no longer merely a local group, but the central knot of a vast international network. Its activities probably cause more travel in and out of Megalopolis than any other enterprise, with the possible exception of the mass media market. The two are, in fact, closely associated.

Manhattan is, of course, the greatest money market, but like other specialized industries, this one, too, has begun to spread. The federal government's increasing involvement in financial affairs has given rise to another substantial financial community in Washington. Other Megalopolitan cities are also increasing in the size and importance of their financial activities. These have become so entangled that Megalopolis as a whole can now be said to play the decisive managerial role formerly ascribed to Manhattan and Boston alone.

Historically, it all grew out of the early overseas trading. But there was also the real estate business, which from its earliest beginning involved speculation and which is now increasingly involved in building development.

Banking often evolved out of the need for specific urban services. One of New York's earliest banks, for instance, grew out of the Manhattan Company, formed in 1799 to provide the city with an adequate water supply.

### Insurance,

too, developed to meet the local needs of the fast-growing cities, such as the risks of fire damage and the risks of the sea—of piracy, barratry, mutiny and shipwreck. Insurance companies soon underwrote both fire damage and overseas trade and added protection against other property and casualty risks. Life insurance began in the 1830's and by 1850 there were forty-eight companies. Such companies are among the large business concerns in America. As a group their investments and loans help regulate the flow of capital in the nation.

On the whole the insurance industry is concentrated in Megalopolis. Its policy-makers and managers often feel the need for close contact with the other members of the financial community.

But this concentration is not necessarily permanent. Younger companies are developing elsewhere, and their rate of growth has been greater than that of the older and larger Megalopolitan companies.

Life and health insurance especially are almost as easy to decentralize as retail trade. Here, too, business follows the customers with agents and scattered local offices.

With the present ease and speed of communications, even the home offices of sizable companies can be set up in any part of the country; and they are bringing to the fore such colorful place names as Wausau, Wisconsin, and Skokie, Illinois.

### The velocity of demand deposits

in a large money market is another reason why the very size of the market causes it to snowball further. The large sums already involved in its operations provide security for further participants. And the speed, or velocity, with which the money is put to use is likely to become still greater.

On the average, a dollar deposited in a Manhattan bank is used just about twice as often within a year as a dollar deposited in one of the banks of the 337 smaller money markets, and Manhattan's velocity still seems to increase.

Always a dynamic process, banking is especially dynamic in the Megalopolitan cities where money rarely lies idle.

Yet cash transfers are only a small fraction of the values actually negotiated. Nor can the money market be separated from the securities market. This, of course, is almost totally dominated by New York with its two stock exchanges. Their clients are scattered over the whole country and abroad. But the "inside" market for securities is believed to be largely in the hands of New York dealer firms, which include the biggest in the country.

### Megalopolis dominates the money market.

Though the statistics have no way of showing it, if all the activities of the New York stock exchanges, New York's other financial activities and those of Washington, Boston and Philadelphia are added together, Megalopolis probably accounts for more than 90 per cent of all financial transactions in the United States.

New glistening, skyscraping palaces of the money market are rising not only around Wall Street and other Megalopolitan downtown areas; they are also invading Park Avenue and the midtown sections of Boston, Philadelphia and even Baltimore.

Their ultimate success depends on two things: the ability of their communities to provide adequate access to them, and the ability of their captains to maintain the vast and complex network of relations which is the essence of commercial organization.

**Money changes hands fastest in Megalopolis**

Megalopolis

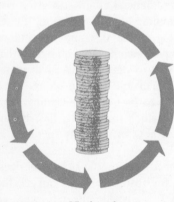

National

# 6 THE JOB REVOLUTION

One of the most important economic developments in our time is the rapid growth in the number of people who make their living not by growing food or making things but by performing services.

The changes this development is bringing about are so drastic that we can call them a revolution, comparable in scope and importance to the industrial revolution.

The trend has been general, but the job revolution is most evident in Megalopolis, which seems to be its foremost testing area.

Back in 1682 Sir William Petty, the English economist, wrote: "There is much more to be gained by *Manufacture* than by *Husbandry;* and by *Merchandise* than *Manufacture* . . ." New England followed this advice. It was the first area where the proportion of workers employed in agriculture decreased, while the proportion of those employed in services—transportation, finance, communications, and personal services—increased. The proportion of those employed in service occupations is now actually greater than the proportion of those employed in manufacturing.

One way to describe this development is to call it, as many economists do, "the expansion of the white-collar labor force." But the term does not entirely fit what is happening. Some of the vastly expanded service industries, such as transportation and utilities, actually employ more "blue-collar" than "white-collar" workers. They also include such classifications as clerical, commercial (including retail and wholesale trade), financial, medical, government work and the special professions (such as law, architecture and designing). It therefore seems more accurate to call this category "the tertiary occupations." This places them neatly in contrast to the primary group of farming and mining and to the secondary group of manufacturing.

### The growth of tertiary occupations

reflects the steady rise in the general standard of living. It is a result of high personal income.

It is also essentially urban and urbanizing.

Office jobs tend to remain concentrated downtown and in midtown although office workers make up the bulk of the suburban invasion of the country. But into the country they bring their urban habits and demands.

For people who work in offices or laboratories live somewhat differently from people who drive tractors or work on the production line.

Their work brings them in constant contact with others, both on the job and at leisure. Their interests are therefore different. They are apt to be more social and more intellectual. They have more means and often the curiosity to read and travel more extensively.

Their different way of life has a profound effect on the economy and on land use.

# Specialization

The larger an organization and the greater the range of whatever it produces, the longer is the chain of specific knowledge and information it will need to collect and disseminate. Each link of this lengthening chain requires a new specialist, or even a new profession.

Such specialists obviously gather where they find a number of organizations to serve. And organizations, as we have seen, obviously like to cluster where they can share the specialists. Hence cities.

And, as we have also seen, once organizations have clustered—be they electronics manufacturers, contract builders, or banks—they will attract more organizations and more specialists.

The specialties then tend to refine themselves and to spawn new sub-specialties. In a very large city, for instance, one may choose from a variety of catering firms, serving a variety of different occasions and different tastes. A small city will have just one or two, since there isn't enough entertaining going on for caterers to specialize.

What is true of caterers is true of truckers or movers as well, to cite an example of a typical tertiary occupation.

It is especially true of what might be called quarternary activities —services that involve transactions, analysis, research, or decision-making, as well as education and government administration. These activities require more training and are better paid.

As the English economist Adam Smith wrote in 1776 in his *Wealth of Nations:* The subdivision of employment in any business "improves dexterity and saves time. Each individual becomes more expert in his own peculiar branch, more work is done upon the whole, and the quantity of science is considerably increased by it."

This is true of other endeavors as well. To quote Adam Smith again: "It is the great multiplication of the production of all the different arts, in consequence of the division of labor, which occasions, in a well-governed society, that universal opulence which extends itself to the lowest ranks of the people."

Adam Smith also recognized that many specialized activities "can be carried on nowhere but in a great town. A porter, for example, can find employment and subsistence in no other place."

**A competent specialist must be educated and trained**
in a much broader area than his specialty. Consider dentistry. A century or two ago, teeth were pulled by barbers. Now dentistry is a separate profession and a dentist must know a great deal about medicine. Not so long ago he did almost all the work his patients' teeth required. Now there are not only a number of sub-specialties but an entire industry producing more and more complex machines and gadgets, chemical materials, artificial teeth and other supplies. A dentist must learn about them, and specialize in a particular line of work to avoid painful blunders. But each of these dental specialists

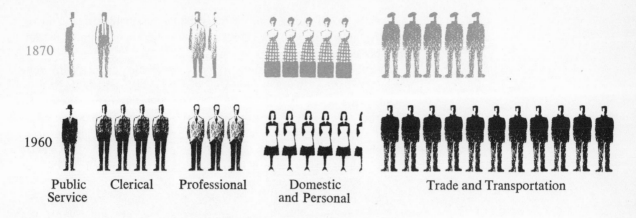

1870

1960

Public
Service

Clerical

Professional

Domestic
and Personal

Trade and Transportation

The relative number of "tertiary occupations" is increasing

still must know as much about the rudiments of his profession as the former small-town practitioner who did all the work himself.

Thus professional specialization is really part of the process of the division of labor rather than specialization in the restricted sense.

### Education is also specializing more and more.

It is hardly possible any longer to teach just "chemistry" or "physics" or "civil engineering." Each of these fields has been subdivided into a whole series of specialties that are constantly being further partitioned. In addition, or perhaps as a result, new disciplines are being established which span the traditional division between formerly distinct fields such as mathematics or biology. At least one university in Megalopolis has recently established a separate department of history of mathematics.

What the students learn is soon reflected in professional life. The government's Civil Service Commission, for instance, now lists 39 different occupations under the title of "engineering." For highways alone, an important new area of vast government expenditure, at least four specializations are listed—highway engineering, highway research engineering, highway design engineering, and highway construction and maintenance engineering.

### Similar specialization occurs in office work.

The number of different white-collar professions has grown along with the increase in the total number of white-collar jobs. This process may continue for some time, for it follows Adam Smith's principle that the size of the market governs the further partitioning of the division of labor.

However, as Adam Smith implied with his example of the porter, continuing division of labor does not depend on the size of the market alone. The market must also be dense enough for specialties to develop, spawn and survive.

Density is, of course, one of the primary characteristics of downtown Megalopolis with its skyscrapers and several thousand inhabitants per acre.

Consider, for instance, the variety of specialties clustered in midtown Manhattan, that bustling area between 34th and 60th Streets. To one side is the Broadway theater and entertainment district. To the other are expensive residences. In the center are huge office towers surrounded by the city's main concentration of hotels, restaurants, department stores, specialty shops, and medical and dental offices. All of them serve a huge number of rather well-paid office workers, wealthy residents and affluent visitors.

There is a great deal of attraction in this unique variety for the kind of employees the offices are looking for, particularly for the young women who make up a large part of the white-collar labor force.

### Urban amenities are essential.

The absence of such urban amenities, conversely, often creates personnel recruitment and morale problems. An insurance company that moved to the suburbs finally had to establish at least some beauty shops nearby in order to enable the company to attract and hold the women employees it needed.

Federal government agencies which have moved to remote areas outside of Washington have experienced recruitment problems they never encountered in the city.

To the problem of finding adequate numbers of specialists *for* the office, then, is added the problem of having adequate numbers of specialists *near* the office—from beauticians to financial and scientific advisors. Herein lies a good part of the reason why 202 of the 500 largest industrial firms in America, listed in the 1958 *Fortune's Directory,* had their national headquarters in Megalopolis.

### Communications are a further factor in the need for concentration.

Office work, of course, is paper work and the papers have to keep moving. The need to move them fast from one operation to another has been given as a reason why these have clustered in Manhattan.

Income from "tertiary occupations" is higher than from manufacturing

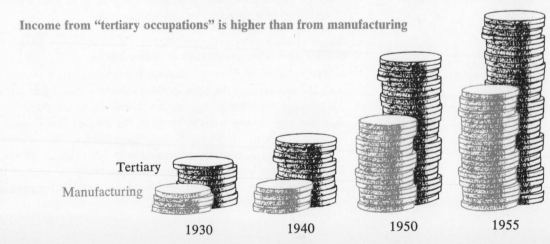

Tertiary

Manufacturing

1930          1940          1950          1955

New York makes most of its out-of-town telephone calls within Megalopolis

In 1959 New York City originated 18 million pieces of mail daily. The volume of mail carried in Megalopolis is astonishing compared to the volume carried over similar distances in other parts of the world.

Communication by mail, however, is often too slow for Megalopolitan office workers. The telephone, therefore, rings with greater intensity than anywhere else, whether this intensity is measured by the number of calls per acre or per inhabitant.

This intensity of telephone calls (see map above) is a fairly good measure of the intensity of social and economic inter-relationships in Megalopolis.

**Offices are also decentralizing recently,**

following manufacturing, trade and services. The big cities therefore no longer employ the same high proportion of the total white-collar labor force as before. But despite decentralization efforts by some government agencies and corporations, the absolute number of office workers in Washington, as well as in New York and Boston, is still increasing.

The statistics can, of course, give no information on the type of offices that move to the suburbs. But it stands to reason that only those offices scatter which do not need either close contact with related organizations or a "prestige location."

Prestige locations are, however, at times outside the big centers, particularly for highly scientific activities. Princeton, New Jersey, has been such a location ever since the early 1940's when the Institute for Advanced Study in that community was joined by the research laboratories of the Radio Corporation of America and the headquarters of the Gallup Poll organization. Other such prestige locations for highly skilled, learned and technical activities are Cambridge, Massachusetts, and New Haven, Connecticut.

# The Cultural Market

The influence of American life of the mass media market in Megalopolis is comparable only to that of its money market.

As the nation's center of broadcasting, book and magazine publishing and the arts, Megalopolis largely determines America's cultural tastes. But its cultural and mass media market does not generate our culture, or even our taste, any more than its money market generates our wealth. What happens, essentially, is that the high velocity of cultural activity in Megalopolis attracts talent from all over the country and the world just as the velocity of money attracts more money. The concentration in both cases adds up to a powerful force which effectively dominates the country.

Again, as with the money market, this is largely due to the fact that Megalopolis has had a head start. While much of the nation looked to the rugged frontier life as the mainspring of the American tradition and the American way of life, the citizens of Megalopolis were not altogether ashamed to read and write books, attend and perform concerts and theater, and enjoy and create visual arts.

When the time came for the rest of the country to follow suit, Megalopolis had the taste-makers and artists, the literary people and producers to establish its cultural predominance.

And that such a time has come is evidenced by the phenomenal and often-cited increase in magazine and newspaper circulation, radio listening, television viewing, and expenditures for books, libraries and museums throughout the country.

### Newspapers

are, of course, the most local of the mass media in influence, content and advertising. But much of their editorial source material is not. They rely a great deal on news and feature agencies which are located in Megalopolis. Local newspaper editors avidly follow the leading Megalopolitan dailies. (Of 86 editors in medium-sized cities in 36 states outside Megalopolis, 93 per cent said they regularly read at least one Megalopolitan newspaper. They gave as their reasons the intrinsic importance of Megalopolis' political and economic power, the wide range of national and international news coverage and the editorials on public affairs.)

### Magazines

are heavily concentrated in Megalopolis not only because of its abundance of writers and artists but also of advertising agencies.

Megalopolis also leads in magazine readership, particularly of the more sophisticated periodicals. It is interesting to note that such magazines as *Esquire, Holiday, Life, The New Yorker* and *Time* are most widely read in Megalopolis, while *Grit* and *True Story* have a greater proportion of readers in other parts of the country.

Increase in national spending for . . .

1929

1950

. . .Books          . . .Theater and Opera   . . .Movies                    . . .Radio and TV

### Radio and Television

broadcasting in Megalopolis exercises its vast influence not through its own stations (only 131 out of a national total of 4,352) but through the networks, the advertising business, and the development and promotion of talent.

The influence that network advertisers and producers exert on the nation's tastes and attitudes far exceeds the influence of any other communications medium.

Most local broadcasting stations have, of course, some kind of network affiliation, as they themselves could not possibly produce the quality and variety of shows necessary to attract and hold advertisers and audiences. All three national networks—CBS, NBC and ABC—are headquartered in Megalopolis. Their activities are supervised by federal agencies. They are further subject to the industry's self-regulatory body, the National Association of Radio and Television Broadcasters in Washington, and are highly influenced by the six "rating services," of which five are located in Megalopolis.

The concentration of networks grew largely out of the already existing concentration of talent. Performers and writers were busy in Megalopolitan theaters, music halls and nightclubs (and journalists and professors were busy in Megalopolitan newspapers and universities) long before broadcasting could develop its own skills.

Only Hollywood can seriously compete with New York in attracting talent. But a Hollywood film must have New York approval before it is fully successful, while a New York production can be a national hit without ever being seen in Hollywood. What's more, Hollywood's movies are mainly financed in New York.

### The performing arts

are also still firmly centered in Megalopolis. People come from all over the country to see the plays on Broadway. Its bright lights are dimmed only slightly by rising theatrical costs and competition from movie and television screens. And if somewhat fewer people crowd New York's theaters, it is because Broadway productions now go on the road more often.

Megalopolis' early start (symphonic music in the United States began with the founding of the Boston Philharmonic Society in 1810) has made it a world center of music. Now that the American public spends more on professional music than on professional baseball, Megalopolis has an overwhelming concentration of famous concert halls, music schools, music publishers, recording companies and booking agents. As a hearing before a Congressional Committee brought out in 1956, this near-monopoly even influences the kind of music the rest of the nation may hear. The selection is largely decided by the tastes of the networks, the recording companies, and the concert bureaus—to say nothing of the central power of the American Federation of Musicians, directed from New York.

### The literary market place

prospers in Megalopolis where so many people have foreign ancestral and cultural backgrounds and cosmopolitan tastes and interests. Here we find not only the majority of the country's publishers but also the bookstores, distributors, literary agents, writers' associations, book clubs and graphic artists.

### The fine arts,

since long before the days of the Medicis, have bloomed most profusely in wealthy cities. Megalopolis, like Florence, owes many of its great art collections and its consequent agglomeration of art dealers to its many millionaires.

It is largely because of names like Frick, Mellon, Guggenheim and Rockefeller that Megalopolis

· has twelve of the nation's sixteen most important museums;

· trains most of the nation's museum directors at Harvard, Princeton and New York University;

· takes up 41 pages in a listing of organizations concerned with art as against only 10 located in such other centers as Chicago, Detroit, San Francisco and Los Angeles;

· publishes ten of twelve leading national art publications;

· and determines the national taste in art ever since the famous International Exhibition of Modern Art at the New York Armory in 1913.

### Advertising

links the cultural market with the money market. Neither could, in our commercial organization, function without it.

About 2 per cent of the gross national income is spent on advertising. And of the ten largest agencies handling this money, seven are located in New York, two in Chicago and one in Philadelphia.

"Madison Avenue" thus sets the style and general tone of most advertising consumer trends and fashions as well.

**Record companies**

Megalopolis    Rest of U.S.

**Important Art Museums**

Megalopolis    Rest of U.S.

**Artists' Organizations**

Megalopolis

**Writers' Associations**

Megalopolis    Rest of U.S.

# Education, Research and Employment

Megalopolis' cultural market attracts and seeks talent everywhere. Its money and commercial markets expect to find talent on the spot. Such enterprises cannot go scouting the country for competent personnel.

This calls for highly specialized, intensive education and research.

Megalopolis' leadership in this field is evident and historic. Its university towns have often grown into corporate training and research centers. These are usually officially independent of the campuses but are nevertheless attracted by the academic environment and stimulus in addition to the numerous and excellent libraries and laboratories.

Libraries of course are easy to account for. Laboratories, however, are statistically elusive because there are so many different kinds. In addition to the training and research laboratories of universities and hospitals, there are many commercial research and testing facilities. They range from large institutions like the Bell Telephone Laboratories and the R.C.A. Research Center in New Jersey to small testing shops found almost anywhere.

The great bulk of the funds for research work comes from the government and some also from private foundations. This does not mean, of course, that all their research and education money is spent in Megalopolis. It is, in fact, put to work all over the world. But here, again, Megalopolis is the center and clearing house of ideas for, and resulting from research in every conceivable field. Such institutions as Columbia University's Teachers College in New York and the National Education Association with headquarters in Washington similarly act as catalysts in the field of education.

## The level of education in Megalopolis

has naturally advanced in this sort of environment. In 1940 there were only a few counties in which more than 30 per cent of those over 25 years had completed at least high school. Only the counties in and around Washington and to a lesser degree Boston showed higher percentages.

Ten years later the suburbs of New York, Philadelphia and Baltimore also exceeded this percentage. By now more than 40 per cent of the adults in or around the major cities have finished high school or more advanced schools. And more than 30 per cent of the adults in practically all of Megalopolis' axial belt are now in this category.

But the big cities and some of their suburbs also showed the highest proportion of poorly educated adults. More than 12 per cent have completed fewer than five grades. Cities embrace both extremes in American society.

The better-educated families who moved to suburbia have been replaced by poorly educated ones, notably among Negroes and Puerto Ricans.

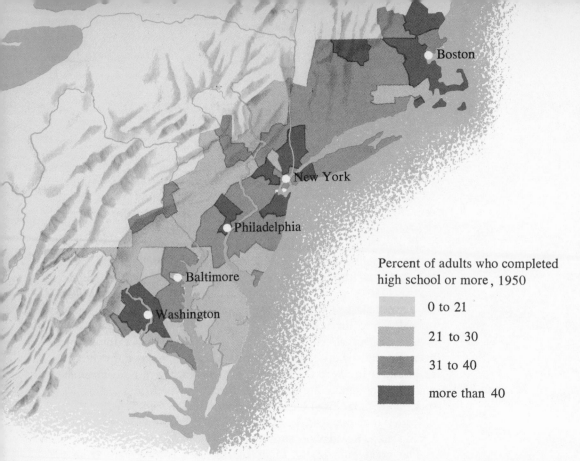

Percent of adults who completed
high school or more, 1950

| | |
|---|---|
| | 0 to 21 |
| | 21 to 30 |
| | 31 to 40 |
| | more than 40 |

The large urban centers have the highest number of well-educated adults . . .

This trend continued in the 1960's. People well know that better education leads to better jobs and a higher income. This, in turn, makes even better education possible for the next generation.

**Very highly literate workers**

are called for in the white-collar revolution. And this makes an upward educational spiral necessary. Although the service industries, like agriculture and manufacturing, are increasingly automated, they also employ more and more highly trained people to operate and service the machines. Banks, for instance, are rapidly mechanizing their operations with electronic devices, including elaborate computing systems. Yet bank employment in the last half of the 1950's increased 65 per cent as compared with an increase of 20 per cent for total nonagricultural employment. And in this field, at least, mechanical equipment is rescuing workers from boring, routine jobs.

Automated mass production, too, does not necessarily reduce all jobs. It hits most heavily the less skilled and the less educated factory workers. To develop and move the mass-produced goods will require more educated research and laboratory personnel, more managers and more skilled secretarial and clerical help.

This is one reason why Dr. James B. Conant in his recent report advocated a "comprehensive high school," large enough to teach at minimum expense all the diverse subjects youth will need to know to keep pace with present and future demands.

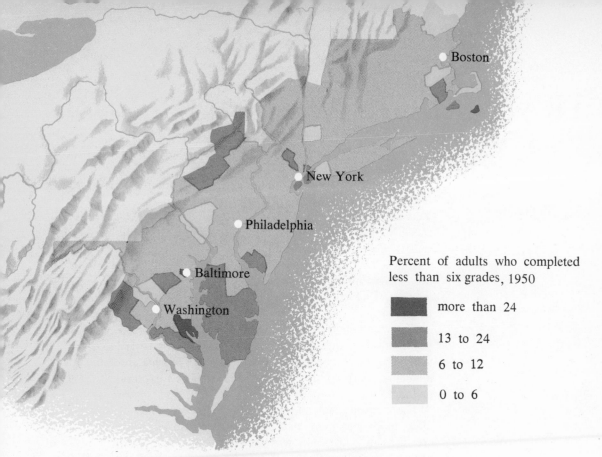

Percent of adults who completed
less than six grades, 1950

more than 24

13 to 24

6 to 12

0 to 6

... but also the largest number of poorly educated people

### The high proportion of women employees

is one of the remarkable features of the white-collar revolution. It has increased considerably in the past decade and is somewhat higher along Megalopolis' axial belt than in the rest of the nation. More than a third of all American females over 14 years of age are now working. They make up 63 per cent of all clerical and sales personnel and 38 per cent of all professional workers.

This demand arises from the growing scale and specialization of business and management. It is met by the growth of cities, which make more women, particularly married ones, available for office work. Urban life makes education easier to come by and housekeeping less time-consuming.

### The boundaries of Megalopolis,

with its high income and high productivity in all fields, coincides neatly with the boundaries of the map showing the degree of education among the population. The contrast between most of Megalopolis and the portions of Virginia beyond Washington's southern suburbs is striking.

The same is true of the map showing the proportion of women in the labor force. Few Virginia counties show a proportion higher than 25 per cent compared with the national average of 29.

Efforts to attract new sources of employment and attain a higher standard of living falter on the threshold of neglected schools.

# 7  TRANSPORTATION

The most vexing and most widely and heatedly discussed problem of Megalopolis is transportation.

Car, truck, bus, subway, railway and airplane traffic is so intense that it places a severe strain on the pocketbook and the nerves. Transportation in Megalopolis is rarely ever moving freely and speedily. At certain points and certain times, traffic is, in fact, snarled almost to a standstill.

The usual vigor and intelligence of the people of Megalopolis and our otherwise so highly successful free enterprise system have failed in organizing efficient transportation, particularly suburban transportation.

The various means of transportation compete fiercely for the rapidly rising demand. Yet this competition seems to succeed only in producing more congestion, poorer service, higher cost and louder demands on the part of the various carriers for more financial aid and facilities.

The conventional and most frequently advanced solution is to build more and more highways and then more and more cars to crowd them. This solution is always easily supported by statistics of need and demand. Neither does it present great technical difficulties.

But the statistics and proposed highway maps never show the ultimate additional fiscal and physical strain on the urban system. They never tell about the human hardships of dislocation and the inordinate amount of expensive and irretrievable waste of space.

The transportation crisis, therefore, is beyond a merely statistical and technical approach. The future viability of Megalopolis depends on more imaginative and more fundamental solutions.

In an area where an inevitably growing population is economically interdependent, smooth and rapid movement of people and goods is a matter of nothing less than survival.

**Number of people carried on a single lane of traffic**

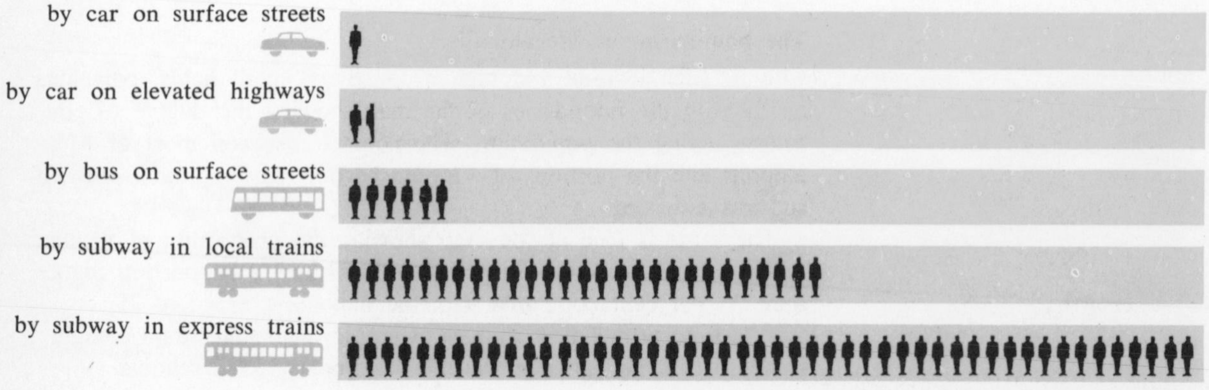

by car on surface streets

by car on elevated highways

by bus on surface streets

by subway in local trains

by subway in express trains

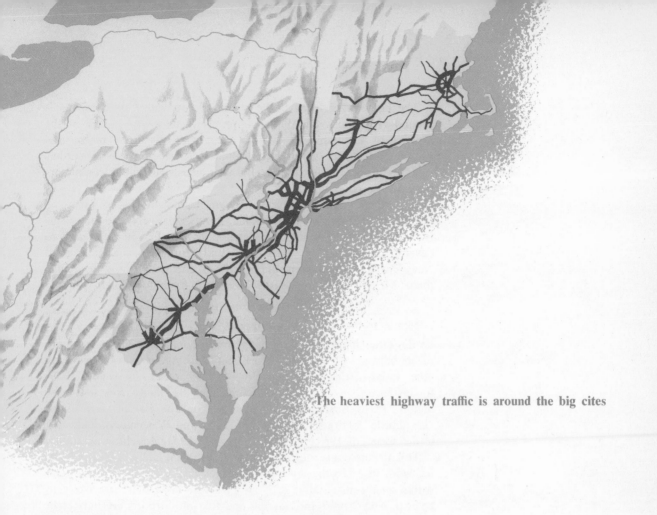

The heaviest highway traffic is around the big cites

# Traffic Between Cities

Other regions in the world—such as the prosperous Amsterdam–Paris–Bonn triangle or central England—are as crowded or even more crowded than Megalopolis. Commuter traffic in the large cities of these regions is just as heavy. But the flow of long-distance traffic is greater in Megalopolis than anywhere else. The reason is, of course, that the cities of Megalopolis are economically far more integrated and interdependent than those of Europe.

Coastwise navigation, moving mainly bulky freight, still remains one of the pillars of Megalopolitan commerce. But most of the goods and people move via highway, rail and air along the region's axial belt, branching out in all directions from the main cities.

### Intercity highway traffic

in Megalopolis is the heaviest in the United States. There is, to be sure, also extraordinarily heavy traffic around Detroit, Cleveland, San Francisco and Los Angeles. California issues more driver's licenses than any other state. But the most heavily traveled distances elsewhere are shorter than in Megalopolis. California's highways, for instance, are not as crowded as those between Boston and Washington.

The heaviest highway traffic concentration within Megalopolis is around New York and Philadelphia. It is relatively lighter in the District of Columbia. Industrial cities with dispersed plants and warehouses attract all kinds of vehicles all day long. Washington's traffic is made up almost entirely of suburban rush-hour commuters heading for government offices and home.

Despite its volume, intercity highway traffic, insofar as it can be distinguished from commuter traffic, moves relatively smoothly. This is mainly due to the fact that Megalopolis was first in the nation to develop a network of "parkways" and "turnpikes." Centering on New York and branching out westward and northward, they have made Megalopolis more easily accessible by automobile.

### Airplane traffic within Megalopolis,

on the other hand, is getting dangerously congested. There are more flights between Boston, New York and Washington than between any other cities in the world that close to each other. In August 1959, for instance, New York airports scheduled 82 flights daily to Washington, 78 to Boston and 43 to Chicago. The Eastern Air Lines' "air shuttle" between Boston, New York and Washington, instituted in the spring of 1961, has further increased Megalopolitan air traffic.

This means dangerous congestion both in the air and on the landing field. In 1956 there were 123 planes in the air at the same time within a fifty-mile radius of New York. In 1975 there are likely to be 350. New York's La Guardia and Idlewild airports are only eight air miles apart and only twice that distance from Newark airport. At times planes must circle a long time over an airport until there is room to land.

### Railroads

seem to have reached the peak of their economic importance and efficiency in the 1920's. Since then they have declined at a rapid rate.

Railroads are at a disadvantage because they are much slower than planes, and not much faster than buses and trucks on express highways and turnpikes. They are confined to their own tracks while motor vehicles can take passengers and freight from door to door with more freedom.

One important reason for the decline of railroad freight traffic is the switch from coal to oil and natural gas as a heat and energy source. National consumption of coal, which was largely freighted by railroads, decreased by 14 per cent between 1930 and 1957. Gas is now moved by pipelines, of course, and oil and its refined products are also carried mainly by pipeline or tanker boats and tank trucks.

In passenger traffic the railroads have lost even more heavily to planes and automobiles, which are both, ironically, powered by petroleum products. But the greater irony of this decline is that railroads, which can move great numbers of people safely at high speed in potentially luxurious comfort, remain the most efficient and natural way to accommodate the flow of intercity passenger traffic.

Passenger trains are still doing relatively well in the West, but in the East, even in Megalopolis, passenger service has been drastically cut despite the great need for it. So many passenger trains have been discontinued in recent years that gloomy prophets predict that by 1970 or thereabouts the passenger train will be a relic of the past. Others disagree with this forecast.

### The sad decline

of the railroads has many reasons. Underlying most of them is the fact that the railroads seem partly unable and partly unwilling to adapt themselves to new conditions and to the competition from automobiles. They thus fail to attract the necessary investment and capable managers. It is a vicious circle.

Railroad management blames the great expense of running passenger trains on the deplorable deterioration and the discontinuation of service. Airlines, it points out, are subsidized, railroads are not. Railroads have to build their own tracks and pay taxes on every parcel of land they use. Motorists get their highways built with public funds and pay no taxes for using them.

The railroads further charge that they are subject to excessive demands of labor unions and to expenses incurred in transporting mail (which, they say, should be carried as freight, using freight stations). Profits, they claim, are frustrated "by archaic regulation, obsolete labor contracts, unequal taxation and publicly sponsored competition." Eastern railroads counter the argument that Western trains seem to do well by passenger traffic by insisting that this is merely a trick in accounting.

If passenger service is to be continued, the railroads say, government subsidies and other help are necessary. Passenger service, they add, should be established as a separate entity, with its own control over revenues and profits.

In Europe, earlier in this century, these same demands led to the nationalization of the railroads. This is, of course, not what railroad management wants and it runs counter to American economic tradition. The nationalized French, Dutch, German, Italian, Swiss and British railroads, however, are successfully meeting the competition from motor cars with swift, clean, punctual train service and modern railroad stations. Many of them accommodate the weary motorist by carrying his car speedily over tedious long distances at reasonable rates while he sleeps, reads or lounges on the same train.

Europe's railroads prove that, properly managed, the railroad is still the most speedy, comfortable, dependable and economical mode of overland passenger transport. What other vehicle can carry two to three hundred people at 80 miles per hour with only 1,500 horsepower and a crew of three to four men?

Two hundred people riding in 150 automobiles, in contrast, use about 15,000 horsepower, or ten times as much energy, plus the energy of their 150 drivers and of the policemen to control them.

Passenger miles

1920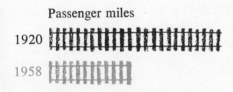

1958

Passengers carried

1920

1958

The disastrous drop of railroad passenger traffic in the U.S.

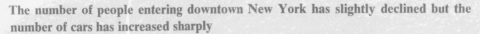

**The number of people entering downtown New York has slightly declined but the number of cars has increased sharply**

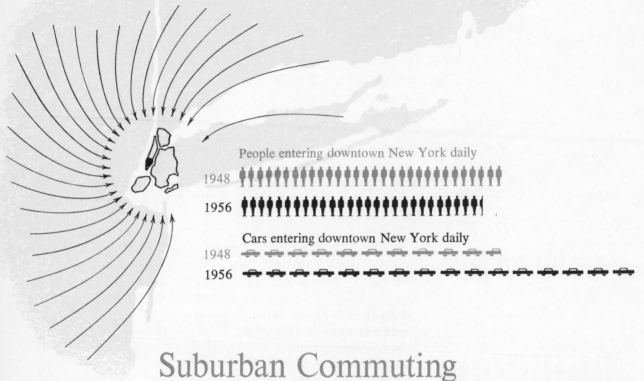

People entering downtown New York daily

1948

1956

Cars entering downtown New York daily

1948

1956

# Suburban Commuting

If Megalopolitan traffic between cities is in a state of crisis, suburban commuting often approaches chaos.

This is not for lack of trying. But to date all of the efforts seem to be on behalf of the automobile. More has been done to keep automobile traffic flowing in and around Manhattan, for instance, than in any other spot on our globe. New highways, bridges, tunnels, garages and parking facilities have been built at great expense and with great abundance.

This has been done, of course, to make it faster and easier for people to drive to work and shop. The result, as the chart on the left shows, has been that more *cars* and trucks enter New York's hub. But the number of *people* entering has declined. Because of the traffic congestion it actually takes people longer to get to work. And the number of shoppers coming into the city has decreased.

This decrease is clearly reflected in the number of people using railroads and subways, which would be the faster, less expensive and more efficient way to carry people in and out.

Congested New York City must move more than three million persons into and out of Manhattan's hub every working day. And half of this traffic ebbs and floods at the same rush hours, from 7 to 10 A.M. and from 4 to 7 P.M.

But in relation to the overall population, other cities have an even larger number of daily commuters. In 1955, 1.6 million of the 1.9 million total population of Washington's metropolitan area entered

96

and left the capital's hub on an average weekday. The reason is that, in contrast to the New York periphery, the Washington suburbs have no significant centers of employment. Washington is a white-collar city where nearly everyone works in a downtown office.

Philadelphia, on the other hand, has fewer white-collar workers and more industry in its suburbs. The commuter traffic to the city's center seems to be stabilized at about half that of Washington. The same is true of Boston and Baltimore. And both these cities share the fate of New York, with its automobile traffic, especially since 1956: As more was done to accommodate automobiles more people used them. Mass transport facilities suffered a substantial loss, and the total number of people working and shopping in the central sections of these cities declined.

The relation between the decay of the central business district and the obsession with building more highways, expressways, freeways and loops into and in the city is thus easy to see. Among the most outspoken advocates for more downtown highways are the merchants in the central business district. They feel the pinch of competition from the suburban shopping centers. But they tend to forget that their problem is to attract more people, not more cars.

Not even a Cadillac, as architect-planner Victor Gruen has pointed out, has ever bought a nickel's worth of merchandise. And bringing cars downtown does little good when for lack of convenient parking the congestion only adds to the confusion and annoyance of downtown shopping.

**Keeping cars out,**

not bringing them into the city, is therefore the problem. Of the traffic approaching a city, only 17 to 32 per cent—depending on its size—have the central business district as their destination. The majority are merely passing through. One way of coping with the motor traffic problem, then, is to build outer belt highways which route this through traffic around the city, not through it. Boston's Route 128, built in 1948, does just that and does it so successfully that other cities, particularly Philadelphia, Baltimore and Washington, are now also building peripheral belt expressways.

The efficient routing of motor traffic within the city is more difficult. Many European cities were ringed by ancient walls. When these were removed they made ideal circular boulevards or what highway engineers now call "inner loops."

In this country most cities are laid out on the checkerboard plan. There are no existing circular routes and to cut them through the existing living organism of the city, as most cities are now attempting, is a painful process. It often involves the tearing down of splendid old buildings, the dislocating of people and stores, and the paving of highly valuable land. The expense in money and human values is enormous. Nor is there any tangible return. Not only must the city pay for the freeways and their maintenance as well as for the necessary additional parking. It also loses tax income from the land that is thus consumed.

Half the total traffic is concentrated at rush hour

Entering city

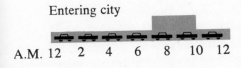

A.M. 12  2  4  6  8  10  12

Leaving city

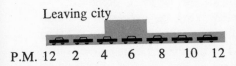

P.M. 12  2  4  6  8  10  12

And the problem of handling downtown motor traffic remains, even when, after much land speculation and political struggling, the downtown loops and expressways are built. Many approaches have been tried: One-way traffic to permit more continuous flow; metered parking; elimination of all parking from congested areas during business hours; and public and private off-street parking facilities. All of this is expensive and none of it fully effective.

### Public transportation

meanwhile is plagued by deficits and neglect. The problem is now being slowly recognized. In Boston, for instance, the bankrupt Elevated Railway Company was turned over to the Metropolitan Transit Authority, a public body, which has maintained and somewhat improved all public transportation. M.T.A.'s decisive step was to extend its rapid transit lines into the suburbs and to provide parking facilities near the stations. This "park-and-ride" system has already succeeded in reducing traffic congestion in downtown Boston by about 7 per cent.

Some slight modernization of New York's rapid transit by the New York City Transit Authority has also had some success. Although there is still an operating deficit, there has been, after a decade of steady decline, a slight increase in passengers in the 1960's.

But the most promising transportation plan to date was launched in Philadelphia in 1958. Under contract with the city, the Pennsylvania and Reading railways provide frequent commuter service to the suburbs at a new, reduced fare of thirty cents. It saves the commuter an average of seventy cents that he would have to pay to operate and park his car. The city makes up for the railroads' deficit.

But the city, too, saves money. Subsidizing the railroads to the tune of about $445,000 a year is proving to be cheaper than maintaining and policing existing highways, let alone building new ones.

The Reading Railway plan has therefore been extended to other routes. The privately owned Philadelphia Transportation Company cooperates by providing feeder buses to the railroad stations and reduced transfer rates to buses and subways downtown. Plans for the future include the electrification of all commuter lines, more parking facilities adjoining the stations, air-conditioned cars, and integration of the new system with the city's other transit facilities. For this the city hopes to receive federal aid.

The only trouble with the Philadelphia program is that it so far stops at the city limits. But there is hope that outlying communities will join in.

These efforts to improve public transportation are, however, meager compared to the huge efforts made on behalf of private cars—at public expense. Commuter railroads, with the exception of Philadelphia, are trapped in a ruinous fiscal squeeze. What little aid they now receive is a pittance compared to the 90 per cent federal subsidies which highways receive. Rapid transit facilities hardly fare better.

The common belief is that automobile transportation "pays for itself." This belief is based on the assumption that the gasoline tax, tolls, and fees paid by car and truck owners bring in the vast sums consumed for building, maintaining and policing highways. This is an error.

The money collected from highway users by the states pays just about what the states themselves spend on their highways. But these state expenditures are heavily augmented by the federal government, that is, from taxes paid by all of us, whether we use highways or not.

The total state and federal expenditure for highways has increased about 123 per cent from 1950 to 1958 while the national income increased only 50 per cent in the same period. The question is whether even the richest country in the world can continue to pay such a disproportionate share of its income on just one of the several means of transportation at our disposal. The question is not, in other words, who pays for what means of transportation. All Americans pay for all transportation directly or indirectly. It is whether the payment is well distributed and whether the present scale of the expense is necessary.

Additional commuter trains are far cheaper than additional highways

Car

Railroad

**Commuting by automobile is far more expensive**

than by public transportation, although the individual motorist is seldom aware of it. He compares only the cost of gas with the price of a subway or railroad ticket. He forgets the price he paid for the car, its maintenance and its insurance, because he would own the car anyway, whether or not he drives it to work. (This is not always true of a second car.) Neither does he think how rapidly his car wears out. He is conditioned to the well-known "built-in obsolescence" and style changes in American cars by which the automobile industry induces him to buy its new models each year.

What the motorist who drives downtown further forgets are the tolls on bridges and expressways, the parking fees and the great waste of his time.

The amount of time given to commuting and even inefficient long-distance transportation has a deep, though difficult-to-measure, effect on people's leisure and their emotional and intellectual performance. Working hours, it is true, have been reduced. So too, thanks to machines and gadgets, has the time we used to spend on many dreary chores. But little of this gain benefits family life, education, cultural pursuits or recreation as long as we must expend it on irritating transportation snarls.

### The public expense of highways,

however, makes such personal expenditures look puny. A comparison of construction costs of highways and railways needed to carry 120,000 passengers per hour from suburbs served by the Pennsylvania Railroad to Philadelphia showed that the ratio was seven to one. Railroad facilities would cost $465 million while highways would cost $3.1 billion.

For 80,000 passengers per hour commuting to the New York metropolitan area from suburbs reached by the Pennsylvania railroad, the ratio of cost was sixteen to one—$283 million as compared to $4,752 million. For both areas combined the savings offered by trains amounted to more than $7 billion.

Yet we cheerfully pay these billions for highways while we begrudge the millions needed to put railroads and rapid transit on an efficient and paying basis.

In many respects the wastefulness of the motor car has been a healthy factor in America's economy. The powerful automobile industry and its related services keeps millions employed and our steel mills and oil refineries going. It would seem, however, that the automobile has now reached its zenith as the most important means of transportation. Its great expense and relative inefficiency as a means of suburban commuting are becoming plainly evident.

There is, furthermore, no telling what changes in our transportation habits technology may bring about. Air transportation is still in the developmental stage. The helicopter is still in its infancy. New rapid transit carriers may hold a lure that our old-fashioned dirty and crowded metropolitan subways now lack.

So it seems rather foolish to keep using so much of our money and valuable urban space for highways as so many Megalopolitan cities seem to be doing.

Transportation planning can no longer be dominated by the interests of one industry alone. It must be closely related to the general planning and renewal of our cities, suburbs and regions as a whole.

Our increased expenditures for highways exceed the increase in national incom

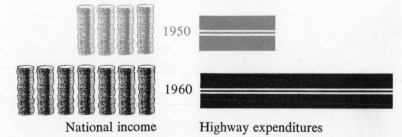

| National income | Highway expenditures |

# 8 LIVING AND WORKING TOGETHER

Look around you in a New York subway or a public bus in Baltimore. Nowhere else in the world is one apt to see such a variety of people of different ethnic, racial, religious and social background.

There are, of course, several cities outside of Megalopolis with a similar hodgepodge of races, but rarely will one find such social variety as well.

Yet, whether they are aware of it or not, the 37 million people of Megalopolis are all neighbors. Their community, both in the tangible and intangible sense, transcends countless administrative, political and emotional divisions.

And while there is a great source of economic and cultural strength in this diversity of people, it also causes many discomforts and difficulties. It calls for constant adjustment and change.

Adjustment is all the more necessary because Megalopolis still continues to attract more people of all kinds, although the rate of its population growth is slightly below the national average. But people in Megalopolis move about more than those in other parts of the country. They are constantly moving in and out of the region.

A good many people who move into Megalopolis are administrators and managers of business and government or other professionals. The presence of these highly paid groups gives Megalopolis the highest average family income in the country. This high average economic standard, in turn, attracts large numbers of very poor people, notably Negroes from the South and Puerto Ricans.

The sharp contrast between rich and poor and the close living together of people of different racial and ethnic origin affect land use and real estate values, schools, the tax income of local governments and the political pattern.

On the whole the people of Megalopolis have learned to cope with the resulting tensions with greater vigor and intelligence than other areas in the country. In recent years, however, these tensions have taken new forms. There are different people involved. New economic needs and specializations have developed. And people must live more closely together than in the past.

We can no longer confine the poor and colored to the city and scatter the white middle class in endlessly sprawling suburbs. Both city and suburbs suffer unless a proper social balance is restored.

It will thus take a great effort on the part of individuals, groups and communities before bigotry, rivalry, and competition fully yield to a recognition of common interests and a loyalty to the high aspirations and promise of the American Constitution and the Bill of Rights.

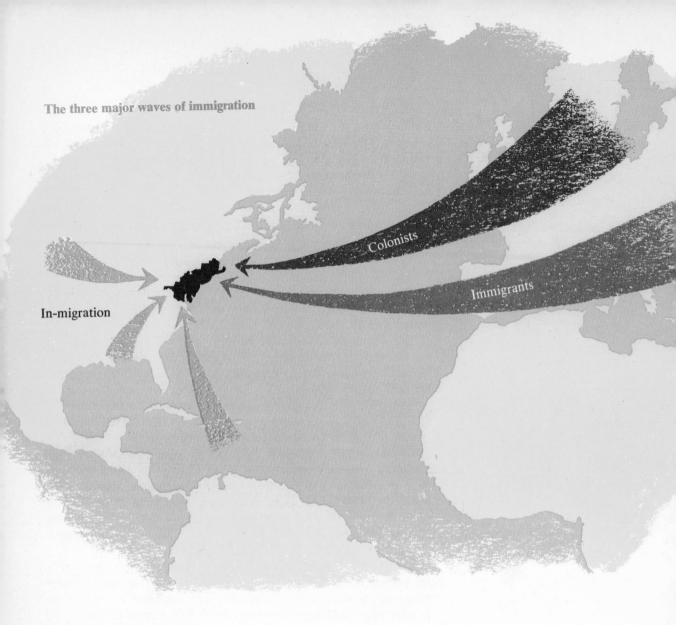

The three major waves of immigration

Colonists

Immigrants

In-migration

# Neighbors in Megalopolis

The people of Megalopolis came in three major waves. First, of course, were the original settlers—British, Dutch, Germans and Swiss, with a sprinkling of Portuguese Jews, French Huguenots and other European refugees. Negroes, brought as slaves to Virginia, Delaware and Maryland, scattered through the rest of Megalopolis, although few of them came to New England or to the hills of Pennsylvania.

Next came the immigrants from Ireland, Italy, and central and eastern Europe and, in New England, from French Canada.

The most recent wave still carries a continuing in-migration of Negroes and Puerto Ricans to the big cities west of the Connecticut River. It adds the need to adjust to racial differences to earlier ethnic, religious and linguistic problems.

## Immigrant groups prefer to remain in Megalopolis,

which has been their traditional place of arrival over the past 300 years. Megalopolis is therefore still the home of 48 per cent of all foreign-born Americans.

One important reason is that the families already settled here often help newcomers from their old country. Immigrants thus tend to cluster together according to their origin and religion. It naturally helps them adapt themselves to the new environment. They also find the cheapest housing in the immigrant neighborhoods.

The Irish first settled mainly in Boston and in New York City where they soon rose to political supremacy. They had the advantage of coming in large numbers and of speaking English. Jewish groups, too, are heavily concentrated in New York and in other large cities.

A few newcomers, of course, followed the lure of the West, often to return a generation or two later rich in skills, money and status. The vast majority, however, stayed in Megalopolis and managed to rise with each generation, first in standard of living and then in social status and education.

In some places and circles they still run up against the social barriers of groups which established themselves earlier. But on the whole Megalopolis now affords all its second-wave immigrants equal social as well as economic opportunity.

Within a relatively short time the newly arrived immigrants can therefore move out of their often-substandard first neighborhoods. They thus make room for later arrivals, a process which, as we have seen, speeds the deterioration of a good many urban districts.

## The distribution of religious faiths

in Megalopolis still shows this tendency of immigrant groups to cluster.

Protestant church membership, surprisingly, is below 20 per cent of the total population in most counties of Megalopolis. Only in Pennsylvania and farther south, and only at a distance from the major cities, does the percentage of Protestants rise above 40 per cent.

The distribution of Roman Catholics is just about the reverse. They predominate in the central cities and in industrial areas, particularly in Massachusetts, Rhode Island and northern New Jersey.

The Jewish group is heavily concentrated in New York City, Boston, Philadelphia and Baltimore and in the nearby mountain and seashore resort areas serving these cities.

After 1930, however, as suburban sprawl set in, middle-class Catholics and Jews moved into rural townships. Here the newcomers were often resented. The question of parochial schools now arises in communities which were solidly Protestant only a generation ago.

The precise extent of this new ethnic and religious "mix" in the suburbs of Megalopolis is difficult to assess with precision. But it seems to be above the national average.

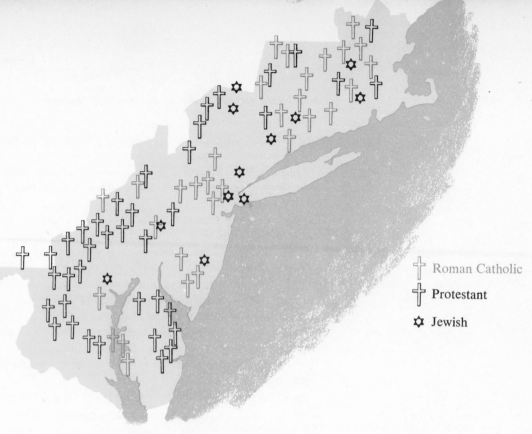

Roman Catholic
Protestant
Jewish

The Roman Catholic migrants still tend to cluster but are moving to the suburbs . . .

### The influx of in-migrants,

that is Negroes from the South and Puerto Ricans, continues in the large cities, particularly in the District of Columbia, in Baltimore and in New York City.

While Negroes in Washington, D. C., and in Baltimore are still largely confined to their spreading ghettos, the Negro population of New York City's Harlem has increased only slightly. Urban redevelopment in Manhattan has gradually pushed the newcomers from the South into the Bronx, Brooklyn and Queens. It still remains difficult for them, however, to find housing in the suburbs although many of them have jobs there. A counter-current at rush hour has therefore developed. Negroes commute out of the city as suburbanites come into it and vice versa.

Puerto Ricans, particularly in New York, have been able to spread more easily over the city. Although 7 per cent of them are classified as Negroes and many more have some Negro blood, they are considered white. They have thus gained access to many deteriorated tenements still closed to American Negroes. In large sections these Spanish-speaking people now dominate the neighborhood.

Yet Puerto Ricans, probably because they are the most recent arrivals and differ in language and culture, generally encounter even more prejudice than Negroes. Their wages appear to be lower. The basic problem in getting good jobs is not only language but the general education necessary for them to adapt to the competitive Megalopolitan environment.

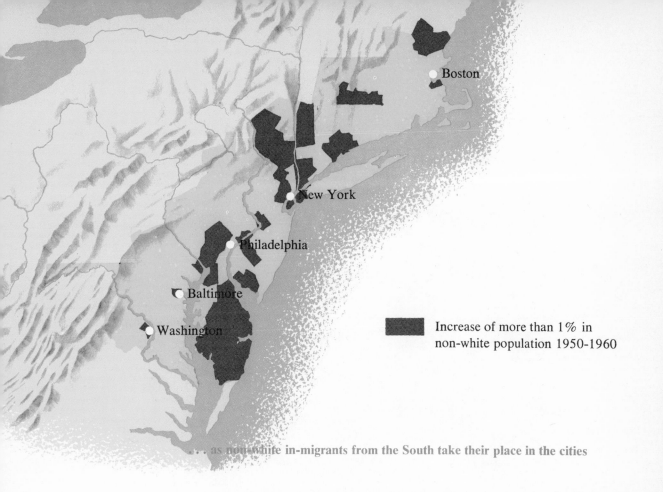

... as non-white in-migrants from the South take their place in the cities

By and large the Megalopolitan cities are further along in the evolution toward equality than the rest of the country, although progress is by no means uniform. There is, for instance, more resistance to school integration in Maryland and Delaware than north of the Mason-Dixon line.

Federal legislation, first sponsored by the New Deal in the 1930's, has somewhat speeded progress toward equal job opportunity. The federal government has, however, only very recently begun a serious attack on discrimination in housing.

Racial and ethnic and religious restrictions on the freedom of people to live where they want is not merely a severe hardship for those discriminated against. It decisively affects the welfare, economic viability and orderly development of Megalopolis as a whole.

The spread of Negro and Puerto Rican neighborhoods causes other groups to move out into the suburbs. Their flight devours precious rural space and contributes to urban sprawl. It also wastes real estate values in the city and speeds their decay.

This, in turn, keeps diminishing the tax income of the city. The vicious spiral grinds downward as reduced revenues lead to poorer public services and schools and thus to more deterioration, crime and unpleasantness, and—more flight to the suburbs.

This happens not only in the very large cities. Newark, for instance, lost about one tenth of its residents between 1950 and 1960. Actually, the proportion of middle-income people who left was even greater. But not all of them were replaced by in-migrants.

105

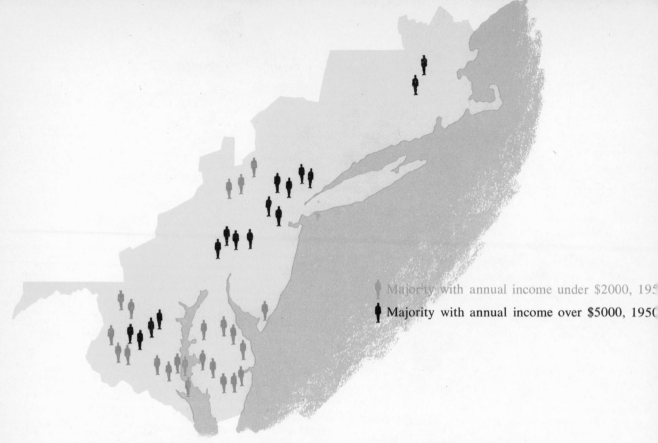

Majority with annual income under $2000, 195[

Majority with annual income over $5000, 195(

The poor cluster in the South and the well-to-do around New York and Washington

The real estate owners are not necessarily unhappy about this. For the average monthly rent paid by Negroes is higher than that paid by whites in the same neighborhoods. Discriminatory rents, however, do not stop the spread of blight and slums.

### Age, income and education

in the city as compared to the suburbs are naturally affected by these changing patterns.

Most people exchange city apartments for more distant and expensive suburban homes to obtain fresh air, greenery and better schools for their children. This is why there are more children in the suburbs than in the cities.

It can be said, in fact, that suburban sprawl was partly caused by the rise in the American birth rate after 1940. The birth rate has now declined a little because fewer people now old enough to marry were born during the depression of the 1930's. But this drop is not apt to last.

The statistics also show that there are more children and very young people south of Philadelphia than north of it. Negroes, particularly in the southern rural areas, and the farmers in the Pennsylvania hills and ridges have large families. Young adults, however, flock to the cities, partly to go to college there and partly to work.

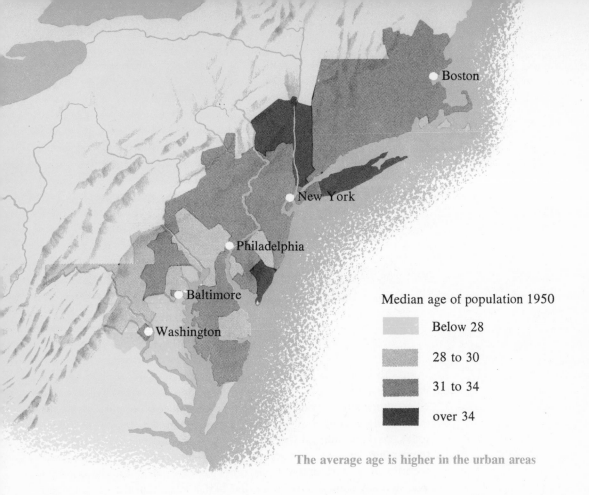

Median age of population 1950

Below 28

28 to 30

31 to 34

over 34

The average age is higher in the urban areas

We can say, then, that while more children are born and brought up away from the urban centers, youngsters spend at least a good part of their life in cities.

But while the average age in cities is higher than in the suburbs or the country, cities are by no means devoid of children. The influx of large Negro and Puerto Rican families has seen to that.

It has also kept the average income level in the cities low, while the high-income rings around them are broadening and thickening. This is, of course, the result of housing discrimination and zoning by which the suburbs manage to keep undesired newcomers out.

This sharp distinction in the income level has a profoundly adverse effect on education both in the suburbs and in the city.

Suburban communities are in a squeeze because they are suddenly confronted with huge numbers of children of school age. Their need for more and better schools and teachers severely taxes their financial resources. Parents who moved to the suburbs largely because of relatively low local taxes now find them rising year after year.

To keep these tax increases down, the communities strive to attract more developments and more industry. These, in turn, bring more children who require more schools, and also more demands for highways, pavements, sewers, lighting, water, parking, playgrounds, hospitals, police and welfare services. The tax burden keeps growing. And the schools hardly ever catch up.

1950

1960

Whites           Negroes

In the cities the financial cycle is even more devilish. City tax income is lowered as the more well-to-do families move out. But the cities must still service these middle-income groups as before, as most of them return during the day as commuters to demand good roads, parking, and all the other public services. In addition it costs them more, of course, to service the low-income groups left to them —more in welfare and various other services. And for the children who actually should have more and better education the schools tend to become worse. There is rarely enough money to maintain adequate educational standards. And this at a time when, as we have seen, employment of almost any kind that would raise their social and economic status depends increasingly on good education.

The end of this vicious circle is not yet in sight. Mere optimism alone will hardly stop it.

### Our much-touted neighborliness,

it seems, still stops short of the homogeneous apartment house project, residential block or suburban development.

Within their own economic and social group Americans are wonderful neighbors, always ready to lend a helping hand and to send out the welcome wagon.

They also take great pride in their tolerance and ability to get along and work with all kinds of people. "All men are created equal," is their solemn credo, "Americans all," their affable boast.

Nor is this ability to make the most of diversity entirely hypocritical. Economically and culturally it has made America and especially Megalopolis what it is—the most affluent and dynamic society on earth.

But it is often apparent only at work.

At home the cosmopolitan American dream turns into a narrowly provincial one. When he leaves his office, store or factory the American yearns for the "right" kind of people in the "right" kind of community. He wants the "right" kind of school and playmates for his children, and the "right" kind of church, club, and even automobile. Americans seem to follow one set of rules on the job and another in the way they live after work.

On the job the Megalopolitan American has made complex diversity a great cultural and economic success. At home this same American retreats behind social walls as strong as any of the old European castles. He stubbornly divorces his cosmopolitan business life from a snobbishly parochial private one.

In spirit the community of his choice is a small, homogeneous world of its own. And if it isn't, he would like it to be.

This spirit is deeply rooted in American tradition: the self-governing township of New England, the self-contained Southern plantation, the settlements of religious sects, the frontiersman's desire for an isolated homestead.

Each of these realms jealously guarded itself against intruding people or influences—even if it was necessary to do business with them.

This separation between the place of working and the place of living leads to the clear-cut distinction between "downtown" and "uptown" and later between the city and the suburbs.

It worked well in the past. There was enough space, even in Megalopolis, for maintaining the "right" kind of community which affords its members status, emotional security and the desired identity in a bewildering world.

It will work well no longer.

New pressures and conflicts have now developed that require increasing integration into one interwoven system. The growing size and density of the population make people and places too interdependent for such easy isolation. The growing needs and the dwindling space and natural resources of cities, suburbs, neighboring counties and states make narrow and exclusive community pride not only obsolete but also destructive.

Community problems can no longer be settled without concern for the larger community of common interests and aspirations.

**The number of eighteen-year-olds will increase sharply**

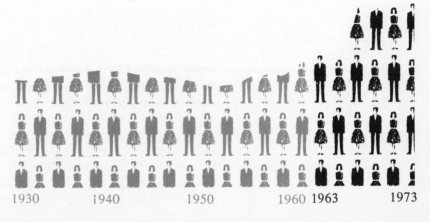

1930      1940      1950      1960 1963      1973

# Sharing a Partitioned Land

The land of Megalopolis is partitioned in many ways.

There are the partitions of geography—the rivers and bays, the ridges and valleys. These have been serious obstacles to communication and traffic in the past. Some of them are still somewhat obstructive because administrative boundaries follow them.

The two rivers bounding Manhattan are a good example. It is physically not much more difficult to bridge and tunnel the Hudson than the East River. But the Hudson divides New York State from New Jersey and tolls are high. Both shores of the East River, on the other hand, are in New York State. Tolls are inexpensive or nonexistent. New York State obviously favors the development of its own territory.

Other partitions are purely administrative, dividing Megalopolis into 10 states and 17 counties. These, in turn, are divided into countless smaller political jurisdictions. The New York metropolitan region, as defined for the purposes of the Regional Plan Association, includes sections of 3 states, 22 counties, and some 1,400 local governments (as against 127 in 1900).

Above these divisions a few interstate agencies are beginning to function. And above *them* hovers the multi-faceted and intricate structure of the federal government.

These partitions are unfortunately not just lines on the map. They represent fierce local pride and clashing rivalry.

The formerly rural and now suburban communities still resent the city, and their representatives vociferously express this resentment in the state legislature. These sentiments have changed but little since the days, 200 years ago, when a "nobleman" compared Connecticut "to a cask of good liquor tapped at both ends, at one of which Boston draws, and New York at the other, till little is left but lees and settlings."

Even the most obvious cooperation between these jurisdictions is often hard to attain, to say nothing of establishing a sensible, integrated system.

How can one expect Baltimoreans to realize their common interests with Bostonians when New York City resents the possible industrialization of Yonkers?

## Competition between jurisdictions

is, however, precisely what has attained the high economic development and integration, of Megalopolis. If conditions for a given industry were not favorable in one state, it moved to another. Wealthy people who work in New York go to live in New Jersey because its tax structure is more to their liking. One need not move far in Megalopolis to find some slight administrative advantage.

Such advantages reaped from governmental partitioning do not last indefinitely, however. Coordination has become essential.

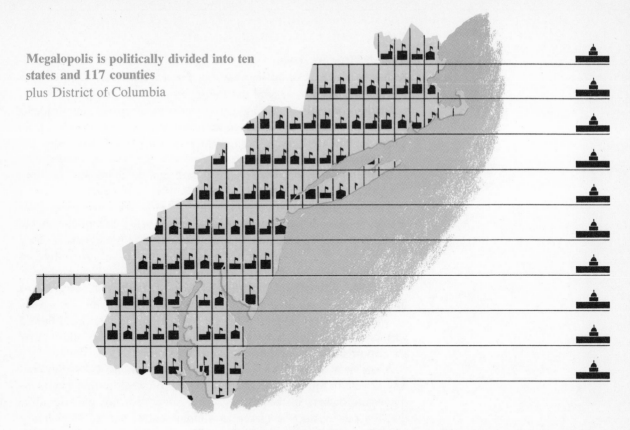

Megalopolis is politically divided into ten
states and 117 counties
plus District of Columbia

But the opposite has happened. The number of local governments in this country has grown from 49,348 in 1952 to 51,833 in
1957. This proliferation is a natural part of the process of metropolitan growth. Unincorporated suburban and interurban areas
gained in population and then incorporated. This, of course, increases the cost of local government. And it is a serious question
whether it is really wise to let government multiply in this manner.

For these new local governments care only about their own do-
main. They usually have a narrow and parochial point of view. They
are often a burden and handicap to the orderly development of
their region and of Megalopolis as a whole.

The question of whether such laissez-faire proliferation of local
self-assertion is really in the best interest of the people as a whole is
not new. It has arisen over and over again in every country faced
with economic changes and the distribution of scarce resources.

The problem of interference versus local autonomy was first raised
at the dawn of history when the Middle East gradually dried up. At
that time the people of the Middle East already had to devise new
laws and new political organizations to assure their survival around
the remaining sources of water. Similar problems produced a Machia-
velli when, at the end of the medieval feudal period, the cities of
Italy grew into great hubs of trade, industry and population. Still
later in history this problem led to the Industrial Revolution in
England in the second half of the eighteenth century.

Essentially, today's problems and challenges are not much different from those of earlier times. Only the terminology and the technical details have changed.

111

## The shortage of space

is among the first problems that call for a cooperative approach. It has aggravated the decay of the central city.

In the competition for industry, recreational space and residents able to pay taxes, the cities have been at a decided disadvantage. Their limited territory is permanently fixed. Yet by their very nature they must admit all comers.

In the countryside, where land is still ample, space and facilities are reserved for local residents and limited uses only.

This naturally forces crowding in the city. Its only alternatives are to build in height or, at great expense, make use of unsuitable land. Portions of the marshes of Hackensack Meadows in New Jersey have thus been put to productive use in a rare effort of cooperation between different municipalities.

Another such instance is Idlewild Airport, built in a marshy area under the auspices of the Port of New York Authority, an agency in which New York and New Jersey participate. Before Idlewild was completed it had become necessary to plan for yet another jet airport to serve the bustling New York area.

A site near Morristown, New Jersey, known as the "Great Swamp" was selected. This choice aroused the ire of wealthy and conservative estate owners in the vicinity. They suggested, not unreasonably, that the new airport be placed in a more central part of New Jersey where it could also serve Philadelphia. But the Port of New York Authority is not concerned with the needs of a Pennsylvania city.

## Water supply

is another acute problem which points up the need for intergovernmental cooperation and coordination in Megalopolis.

The average American uses 200 gallons a year just to quench his thirst and another 15,000 gallons for washing, laundering, heating, and disposing waste. Megalopolis' specialized farming and its suburban lawns and gardens also use great quantities of water. Last but not least there are the huge needs of industry, particularly for steam to generate electric power.

Rainfall is usually plentiful all year. From the hills to the north and west many good-sized streams flow across Megalopolis and there are stable ground water supplies at small depths.

Because of inadequate supply facilities or periods of drought or both, the major cities are nevertheless threatened with water shortages. To meet present and anticipated needs they must reach farther and farther into the hinterland.

But this hinterland must be shared by many cities, and each feels itself threatened and its future jeopardized by the needs of a thirsty neighbor.

New York City is the thirstiest of them all. Its local sources are very limited. It first reached out to Westchester County, then to the Catskills and finally to the upper basin of the Delaware River the Cannonsville Reservoir.

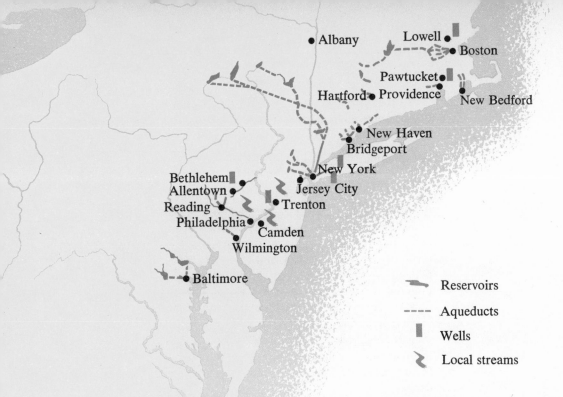

Inter-city cooperation is needed to assure adequate water supply

New Jersey and Pennsylvania, downstream of the Delaware, felt threatened. Long litigation ensued. The eventual result, after twenty years of hassle, is an interstate compact which set up the Delaware River Basin Commission, representing Delaware, New Jersey, New York, Pennsylvania and the federal government.

But to date such cooperation is rare in Megalopolis. Boston, for example, reaches westward beyond Worcester and close to Springfield for its water. Springfield and Hartford compete for the same watershed. New York has gone far into the hinterlands of northern New Jersey and even of Trenton and Philadelphia. And if Philadelphia wanted to draw more water from the Schuylkill River it would find Reading in its way.

Surely this is an expensive way to meet a basic need.

Nor is such competition limited to the large cities. The local scramble is well illustrated by the utterly complex and largely uncoordinated water supply system, both public and private, in New Jersey. Both water and public funds are wasted by the desire of every community to have its own supply. Indeed, many people rely on their own wells. An attempt at coordination during World War II ended when the war did.

Water is one example—and a good one—of entanglements and complexities of neighborhoods in Megalopolis.

Besides competing with others for their increasing needs, communities must decide how much they are willing to spend, how to regulate consumption to save both water and money, and what quality of water to supply.

All this involves such matters as controlling pollution, treating the water supply and—local politics.

## Air pollution

presents similar problems. It illustrates how uncontrolled and unplanned urban sprawl not only has economic and aesthetic consequences but also affects human health and safety.

The dense accumulation of innumerable cars, power houses, manufacturing plants and other sources of poisonous exhausts and smoke obviously requires checks and controls. But effective controls are difficult or impossible in an administratively over-partitioned land. Polluted air does not respect political boundaries.

New York City and Philadelphia, for instance, can blame much of their polluted air on their next-door neighbors in New Jersey, although neighbors are often accused of nuisances that should first be taken care of at home. There is now a joint New York and New Jersey Interstate Sanitary Commission attempting to cope with this danger.

In general, however, lack of regional air-pollution controls and zoning regulations remains a serious obstacle to the best efforts to improve the air Megalopolitans breathe.

Here, as in other areas—such as milk supply, transportation (particularly aviation), and civil defense—people look increasingly to the federal government to exert coordinating authority. Those who object to federal "interference" with "states' rights" might well ponder the fact that increased federal power would not be necessary if the states would only learn to cooperate more effectively with each other.

Such cooperation must face up to three main problems: financing, the planning of orderly growth, and, most important, the opening up of new channels of coordination between neighboring jurisdictions of all levels of government.

## Financial difficulties are constantly increasing.

Local government has become big business. Both budgets and the number of employees have rapidly grown in the twentieth century and so has the indebtedness.

The expenditures of local government in recent years have far surpassed those of state governments.

Yet local revenues are inadequate to cover local expenditures. The local governments have therefore turned to the state's treasury for a share of the funds collected from state taxes.

The states, in turn, receive financial help from federal funds.

In this fiscal doubleplay, state and federal contributions combined make up 26 per cent of all local revenues.

The local authorities are, however, somewhat limited in their freedom to spend this good quarter of their income. Congressional and state legislation earmarks it for specific purposes such as highway construction, public schools, hospitals, health and other services.

114

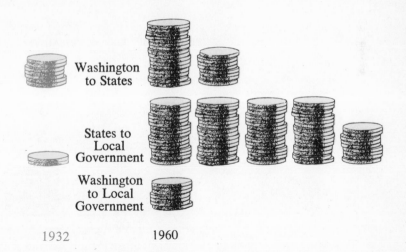

Washington to States

States to Local Government

Washington to Local Government

1932          1960

In the past 25 years outside aid to local government has increased more than eight times

Another limitation on a locality's freedom to dispose of its budget is the fact that much outside help is given to supplement specific programs. Thus localities often launch such programs to get the assistance even though some other venture might be more important.

The extent of outside aid granted local governments varies considerably and bears no relation to actual need. The reason is that in most state legislatures, notably those of New York, Pennsylvania and Maryland, the rural areas have long held the balance of power. Rural communities are therefore receiving far more aid than their share of the state's population warrants.

Nationally speaking, school districts fare best. On the average they receive 43 per cent of their revenue from outside sources. Counties follow closely with 38 per cent. Townships depend on grants and shared taxes for 25 per cent of their funds. But cities obtain only about 14 per cent on the average. The larger the city the smaller the percentage of outside help it receives.

Although these are national ratios, the implications for Megalopolis are clear. Neither the large central cities nor the metropolitan areas are receiving a fair share of the financial help they desperately need.

The central cities need it because they are losing resident population but must still provide services for commuting and visiting outsiders. And the metropolitan suburbs need it because their great influx of new residents require more and more costly services spread over an increasingly sprawling area. They try to expand their tax base by attracting more people and industry. But to serve these they must, of course, first invest money in new schools, roads, and sewers. The return on this investment in the form of additional tax comes in much later.

Despite federal aid, state and local taxes are therefore constantly going up. Inequities and difficulties arise. One is that some Megalo-

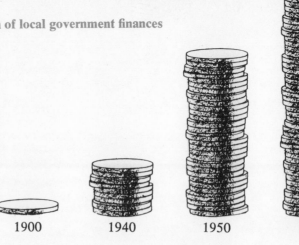

Growth of local government finances

1900    1940    1950    1960

politan states have an income tax which they levy not only on their own residents but also on incomes earned by people who live in another state. Another is the distribution of state-collected tax money to the cities.

New York State, for instance, assigns New York City a share of its revenue, according to the city's proportion of the Census population. Since that population has been declining, the aid the city receives is also shrinking. However, expenditures for urban renewal, education and welfare must, of course, be increased if the city wants to arrest even further population losses.

Cities are centers. That means they must serve a wide area around them and not just their own residents. Their well-being affects the entire surrounding area, transcending state lines, just as the heart affects the health of the entire body.

Cities are furthermore expected to provide not only the necessities but such institutions as parks, zoological and botanical gardens, museums and libraries, which do not bring any revenue but cost a great deal.

This is particularly true of Washington, D. C., which, as the national capital, must serve the entire nation. The whole nation must therefore share in the cost of its efficient operation.

The revenues American cities can raise on their own are entirely insufficient to meet these responsibilities. They rely almost exclusively on the property tax. The proportion of income from this source has recently been declining. New sources have had to be developed but such new taxes and fees have so far failed to solve the problem.

Proposals to increase this tax, as land values increase, would bring little relief. For the large cities which have the greatest need for increased income also have the highest proportion of tax-exempt property.

In New York City, for instance, more than 30 per cent of all real property belongs to the city itself or to other tax-exempt institutions. This includes parks, schools, public buildings, public works, public housing, sewerage systems, hospitals, harbor piers and airports. Other properties are tax exempt because they belong to the state or federal governments or to religious, educational, philanthropic and

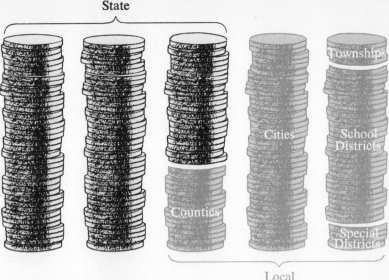

other non-profit institutions. In Boston this percentage is even higher
—36.2 per cent. In Providence it is 24 per cent, in Philadelphia 22
per cent, and in Baltimore 18 per cent.

There is no question that the limits of local taxation have been
reached. The urbanization and economic integration of Megalopolis
make more state and federal aid to its large centers imperative.

### Metropolitan planning and administrative coordination

is being attempted, of course, but as yet on a totally insufficient scale.
In one way or another Megalopolis has so far only muddled through.
It seems, as Albert Einstein has said, that "politics is more difficult
than physics."

Coordinated planning and administration has therefore to date
been almost exclusively confined to narrowly specialized activities.
Spanning administrative boundaries are fire protection districts, soil
conservation districts and drainage districts. There are also special
"authorities" for the construction and operation of toll roads and
bridges, port and airport facilities, and other such common tasks.

These districts and authorities are helpful, of course. They also
point up how poorly other government units cope with problems
arising from regional integration.

The port authorities of New York, Massachusetts and the Delaware River are examples of good cooperative efforts. So is Boston's
Metropolitan Transit Authority and the Waterfront Commission of
New York Harbor, set up to control labor conditions on the docks
and eliminate racketeering.

Another way of meeting these problems is by annexation of neighboring communities. Baltimore annexed large suburban areas in this
fashion back in 1918. And New York City grew by annexing Brooklyn and the Bronx.

Consolidation is another method. The city and county of Philadelphia were consolidated as early as 1854. The present boundaries
of New York were established in 1898 by a combination of annexation and consolidation.

Both these methods have obvious limitations. They cannot extend
a city's area indefinitely. Nor can they transcend state lines.

117

Cities

Townships

Counties

School
Districts

How outside help to local
government is distributed

Federal &
State Aid

Sales tax
license fees

Utilities,
insurance
trusts, etc.

Property tax

The revenue of cities

A far better method is to establish a metropolitan government like that developed in Greater Toronto, Canada, and in Dade County, Florida. It would not solve all the problems in Megalopolis, however, for many of them affect regions larger than one individual metropolitan area.

New York made a start in this direction when the Metropolitan Regional Council was established in 1956. It consists of a voluntary association of the top elected officials of twenty-one counties, twenty major cities, and other governmental units in New York, New Jersey and Connecticut.

Among the topics the Council has discussed and in some cases acted upon are transportation and traffic, parks, water supply, water and air pollution, civil defense, and juvenile delinquency.

As Victor Jones, a specialist in local government has observed, however, there is less talk about metropolitan government today than there was before World War II. Instead, current efforts tend towards federation and specialized agencies and authorities. "There must be a community before there can be effective and stable government," Jones says. In law and in fact the existing local governments are still creatures of all the political forces we call state governments.

Another expert, Luther Gulick, chairman of the Institute of Public Administration, says: ". . . we know that there can be no effective attack on the rising problems of the metropolis without a comprehensive and cooperative attack."

Concern solely with municipal government or planning or transportation or any other single aspect of Megalopolis' growth and challenge is no longer sufficient. The present administrative boundaries are dissolving. New political frameworks must emerge which reflect political and economic realities.

# 9 THE CHALLENGE OF MEGALOPOLIS *

It is too early to speak of a "Megalopolitan community." Perhaps such a thing will never come about. There is more competition, rivalry and diversity among the people of Megalopolis than common loyalty or recognition of common interest.

In many respects this is good. Competition and diversity account for much of the area's great strength and wealth. It has contributed to phenomenal growth in the number of people, their material productivity and their scientific, technical and cultural accomplishments.

This growth is bound to continue, if not accelerate. But it will continue within strictly prescribed geographical limits. The eastern seaboard of the United States cannot expand, of course. It will only become increasingly more urbanized and densely settled. To date, this dynamic process is, however, all but totally unplanned and helter-skelter.

With its many blessings this spontaneous combustion has also created many serious problems.

Some of these are problems of human adjustment to a completely new way of life. For most people, living in Megalopolis today is as different as traveling in a stagecoach is from flying in a jet airplane. There is constant mobility, a constant need to get along with different groups of people, a constant need to acquire new knowledge and understanding—in a word: constant social change.

This change has a profound impact on accustomed ways of family life, on social and aesthetic standards, on morals and values.

Other vexing problems concern the physical functioning of the Megalopolitan environment. Undreamed-of advances in science and technology have coincided with undreamed-of advances in the standard of living of most though not all of the people in Megalopolis.

**Great strides have been made**

in conquering disease, reducing infant mortality and prolonging human life. Human toil and working hours have been considerably reduced and potential leisure time has been correspondingly increased. The automobile has given people the freedom to go just about wherever they want. More people than ever before have what the U.S. Housing Act of 1949 calls "decent, safe and sanitary housing." And most Megalopolitan homes, with their modern heating and air conditioning, their refrigerators and other conveniences, have a degree of comfort that people in other parts of the world rightly consider luxurious.

But when the people of Megalopolis step out of their homes and apartments, whether they are fully aware of it or not, they often find

* This chapter has taken advantage of many thoughts and observations expressed by Jean Gottmann in an essay entitled *Economics, Esthetics and Ethics in Modern Urbanization* published as a by-product to his *Megalopolis* by the Twentieth Century Fund, 1962.

themselves in an environment so inefficient and so polluted with ugliness that one foreign observer has called it "the mess that is man-made America."

Our gains in health are imperiled by smog, air pollution, lack of conveniently accessible outdoor recreation and playgrounds, and the hazards of uncontrolled automobile traffic. Our gains in leisure time are imperiled by long, tiresome and unproductive hours of commuting to work. The joys of automotive mobility are severely dampened by traffic jams and parking difficulties. The increased comforts and beauty *in* our homes are largely offset by the lack of amenities and beauty in the cities, suburbs and along the highways *around* them.

The impact of all this on people has created a new concern, so new it has required a new expression—the concern for "mental health." Mental disease, of course, has probably always existed in various forms. But mental health as a general social problem has never existed before our time. It has become important now because the dynamics of Megalopolis would adjust people to a changing environment rather than adjusting the environment to the people.

The environmental problems of Megalopolis are slowly beginning to be widely recognized. And just as diagnosis is the first essential step toward cure, so is popular recognition of a problem the first essential step toward its solution. But it is only a first step.

Nor are the problems of livability in a dynamic, urbanized environment confined to Megalopolis. The whole world is in a period of accelerating change. The process of urban growth in our time is a source of troubled concern for many communities and governments. It has become so rapid and ubiquitous as to overshadow most other modern problems.

### "Con-urbation,"

as the British call the growing together of cities, is happening, as we have seen, on both coasts and elsewhere in the United States. In Western Europe, too, cities are beginning to grow and grow together by leaps and bounds. Even in the relatively stagnant economies of Spain and Portugal cities are expanding. And in Communist-dominated countries and the underdeveloped lands of Asia, Africa and South America, too, commercial development, industrialization, mechanization, motorization and automation are changing the old rural order into an urban one.

In all these countries and regions the process of urban growth develops along specific lines, most of which differ from place to place. Each community has its own variety of these worldwide problems and each has or must find its own ways and means of tackling them. Local characteristics must be respected. But it is always helpful to learn how others are coping with a general trend.

Thus much of the world looks at the precedents set and the experiments tried in Megalopolis. Here both the blessings and the perils are most concentrated and most intense. Here—so both America and the rest of the world have a right to hope—is the leadership. And here

The birth rate still keeping going up

1935  1940  1945  1952  1958
                        -57   -60

120

—if America and the rest of the world are not to be disappointed—must evolve, if not a "Megalopolitan community" in the political sense, at least a Megalopolitan community *spirit*.

There is no doubt that with its affluence, Megalopolis has the means, and that with its unprecedented concentration of learning it has the wisdom, to meet its environmental problems. It now needs the will to do so.

### Comprehensive regional planning

to guide the development of Megalopolis and assure its livability is the great, over-riding challenge. We have planning for small units such as city and suburban neighborhoods and urban renewal projects. But these pieces do not yet make a clear, workable and attractive mosaic. Nor is comprehensive regional planning of much use if it remains a theoretical exercise confined to study groups, commissions and boards with insufficient political and popular support to make it effective. Such support, in turn, requires the will and the spirit of the community.

To date this has been wanting. Until now our faith in ever-expanding consumption to the point of conspicuous waste has achieved ever-expanding production. This cycle has thus been a constructive factor in economic growth. Our affluence is based on it. As a nation we have learned, however, that we cannot continue indefinitely to waste our natural resources. We are beginning to guard our wilderness, our forests, our water and our mineral resources. We are carefully planning their use even if this means curbing unlimited, *laissez-faire* free enterprise.

Now we must learn to guard and plan the use of our land and of our urban resources. We can no longer afford to let urbanization run rampant over our countryside. Nor can we continue to tear down sound buildings merely because some new use of their site may appear to be more profitable. Quick individual gain often means an irretrievable, permanent loss to the community.

Yet, there is no instance, anywhere, of successful, comprehensive planning of a wide urbanized region. Cities in other countries, particularly Paris and Moscow, have attempted to control metropolitan growth. Neither city was able to check the influx of population. Restrictive measures only contributed to worse congestion, especially in housing.

Perhaps the planning by the Dutch government for the distribution of population and industries in Holland is the closest any effort has come to providing for people's needs while at the same time preserving the landscape. But no other authority has yet managed to reconcile the immediate pressures and interests of individuals and local communities with the long-range interests of the general welfare. This applies to such matters as water, air and land pollution, water and energy supply, sewerage, desirable housing for low-income and minority groups, recreation and public transportation.

The cause of comprehensive, regional planning is not served by purely emotional and negative criticism of urban sprawl. It is true

121

that the dispersal of city functions depletes and impoverishes the city and despoils the countryside to the great detriment of people who live in either place. But urban dispersal of many city functions, such as manufacturing, wholesale warehousing and housing for workers, is inevitable. So is the desire of most Americans to own a house and a yard of their own in a suburban setting, no matter how far from their place of work.

Neither is the cause of planning for order and livability served by the claim that dispersal of *all* city functions is inevitable. It is tempting to dismiss concentrated cities as obsolete. It is easy to argue that modern transportation and communication by television, telephone, teletype and electronic devices yet to come make it unnecessary for people to cluster in large, compact communities.

But these arguments are wrong.

As we have seen, the great economic and cultural strength of Megalopolis came from its burgeoning cities. And the great economic and cultural strength of the cities came from their dense concentration of a variety of skilled, talented and enterprising people. Such individuals also live in dispersed rural communities. But it is the continuing, spontaneous, face-to-face contact of city dwellers that throughout history has built civilizations. Such personal, spontaneous human contact can hardly be replaced by electronic communication devices.

Throughout history the city has been the dominant center of wealth, authority, responsibility and cultural attainment. When great cities went down, the cultures they created went down with them —Babylon, Carthage, ancient Athens and Rome.

The city as an institution, however, has remained invincible to this day. For every great nation, every great civilization, every culture which succeeded the great city-states of antiquity again culminated in great cities. Italy's great contributions to modern civilization are unthinkable without Rome and Milan. So is France without Paris, England without London, or the United States without the great cities of the eastern seaboard.

Today there is a danger, however, that the cities of Megalopolis and of similar con-urbations elsewhere are losing their identity and distinction. With urban functions and living habits sprawling all over the countryside, there is nothing special any more about the city itself.

The appearance of city and countryside are becoming increasingly alike, standardized and uniform, and so are the lives of their inhabitants. People as well as their environment are in danger of losing their individuality, their local tradition and their sense of history.

The objectives of regional planning, then, should be neither to attempt to reverse an inevitable, dynamic trend, nor merely to sanction it. The threats of the future can only be met by finding the valid patterns in the present disorderliness and, with new, creative thought, give them order and meaning.

We must decide what an urban community should be, what kind of cities, suburbs and countryside we want.

### Freedom of choice

for all people to live as and where they wish would seem what we want most in a democratic society. It is the fifth freedom we should consider essential. Some will want to live in townhouses or high-rise towers within walking distance of their place of work in the lively bustle of the city. Others will want to live in a garden-city environment where their children can roam and play in the safety of private yards. All Americans will want to preserve our great outdoors, some unspoiled countryside, and have easy access to it.

If this is so, it shouldn't be hard to agree that we limit peoples' choices if they are forced to forego either a desired job or a desired home environment because the distance between the two is too great. We limit free choice if we do not offer desirable housing for middle-income people in the city or for low-income people in the suburbs and if we permit both the bustling city and the tranquil suburbs to deteriorate through chaotic dispersal.

The opposite of dispersal, of course, is concentration. And a greater, more concerted effort at concentrating proper and economically feasible city functions in the city would seem to be imperative. The central city in Megalopolis has, as we have seen, declined. Federally assisted urban renewal is lately attempting to help arrest this decline. But this effort is balanced, if not offset, by simultaneous federally aided programs, such as easy mortgage insurance for suburban homes and highway construction, which accelerate dispersal. Centripetal and centrifugal forces are supported by the same government at the same time with equal enthusiasm. We spend a lot of money to help lure middle-income people back into the city and at the same time we make it cheaper and easier for them to live in the suburbs.

It is probably a good thing for the city to lose manufacturing plants and warehouses. But it cannot afford also to lose its offices and with them its economic base and reason for being.

The present trend is towards the clustering of large new offices downtown. But the central city is beginning to get some competition

Expansion of office space in the U.S.

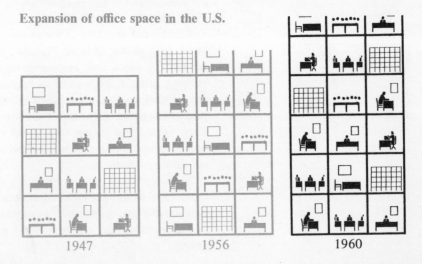

1947          1956          1960

from the suburban ring. In Philadelphia, for instance, suburban office space is heavily competing with downtown office space. In Washington the federal government has only very recently reversed a trend to locate large federal agencies far out in the Maryland and Virginia countryside.

To hold offices and with them white-collar workers, retail stores, restaurants, theaters, museums, art galleries and all the rest, the city must again become attractive and accessible. It must win the battle against blight and the invasion of the automobile.

We need to take a new look at the present system of property taxation which encourages withholding urban land from needed uses for speculation. This discourages the improvement of existing property. To save the city means finding ways to stimulate more and better housing for people of moderate income. Slum clearance is not enough. We need a comprehensive program of slum prevention. Nor are more and more freeways and highways the only answer to the city's transportation problem. They simply bring more cars into the city, which, in turn, increases the demand for still more highways and, of course, more parking spaces. This takes valuable and needed housing, park land and income from taxable land away from the city and requires maintenance expenditures to boot. The city must then resort to higher taxes, subsidies or both.

Subways and other forms of rail transportation are, as we have seen, far less expensive and far more efficient. They must now also be made more attractive for cities to finance and for commuters to use.


### Man's need for beauty

must also be considered in attacking our urban problems. The city can and should be a work of art. Ethics demand, for instance, that we give first priority to housing low-income people. But there is no reason why we can't at the same time try harder to meet our esthetic needs and make low-income housing attractive. Esthetics are not in opposition to the ethics of urban planning and redevelopment. Combined they can yield handsome economic and social benefits.

Much land inside a city can be turned into green belts, avenues, parks and plazas if most transportation is channeled underground. In many cities lovely pedestrian plazas are built over underground parking garages. This trend should be encouraged. We should reserve the ground level for people who walk and children who play and give them more greenery, fresh air and less noise and confusion. Cars, buses and trains should be put in tunnels where they have unobstructed traffic movement. We must separate men and machines on our city streets.

The techniques of tunneling are rapidly progressing. If it pays to build tunnels several miles long under high mountains to shorten the road from Paris to Madrid, from Geneva to Turin, and from Zurich to Milan, it would surely pay to make our American cities more livable.

American architecture today is probably outstanding in the world. It has created numerous handsome office towers, corporation palaces and cultural centers. But architects have lavished their talents mainly on such prestige buildings, much as architects in former days created their greatest works of art to enhance the prestige of princes and the church. Modern architects are just beginning to turn their attention from individual architectural showcases to building projects and clusters, to the spaces between buildings and the design of streets, avenues, plazas and neighborhoods, in short to urban design. In their attempts to make whole sections and neighborhoods of the city harmonious and beautiful, they need greater support from the public and the authorities who all too often feel that good design and embellishments such as fountains, statues and attractive landscaping are "frills" and luxuries.

In this century of the common man and of an increasing popular appreciation of the arts, it seems sad, moreover, that our housing projects, public schools and public buildings are generally still among our least attractive buildings. Our architects, as many privately financed buildings and our embassies abroad have shown, can do far better. But good architecture needs not only good architects but also understanding clients. And most housing developers and government bureaucrats are slow in catching up with a public taste that is increasingly becoming more sophisticated.

### Regional planning needs regional support.

These are no longer just problems of the city alone. The city, as we have shown in these pages, is increasingly interdependent with the rest of the complex living and working environment we have called Megalopolis. If the city is to be attractive or even beautiful it must achieve the proper concentration of some economic and social functions and the orderly dispersal of others. It must maintain a balance of inhabitants of all income groups. It must bring order into its chaotic traffic conditions.

Each office building in the city, to be prosperous, must be conveniently accessible to the people who work there, many of whom live in the suburbs. Each new freeway in the city means tearing down homes and displacing people, and often the most efficient way to re-house them is beyond the city limits. Mass transportation cannot work unless the suburban commuters who use it are sufficiently concentrated in the vicinity of each station to fill the fare box.

All this means that planning in and for the city is of very limited use unless it is thoughtfully coordinated with the entire region surrounding it.

One prerequisite of such effective regional planning is that new legal and administrative procedures must now be set up to follow the new housing, social and economic patterns already established. The obstacle to such regional organization, or at least effective cooperation, is the great number of local governments. But we should not be too impressed by local administrative boundaries and the loyalties they inspire. These loyalties were never meant to supersede the loyalty and devotion of Americans to the common welfare.

Like any concerted effort for the general welfare, orderly planning and building, new policies of credit and taxation, the organization of a balanced metropolitan transportation network, essential controls of land use and housing distribution, and esthetic controls over unrestricted advertising, incompatible structures and other forms of ugliness, will not meet with the approval of all. Such an approach will upset accustomed ways of thinking and acting. In the lucrative real estate business it may curb individual profit. Some people still consider such things "undemocratic."

But in the end the American people have always chosen the best course to "provide for the general welfare, and secure the blessings of liberty to ourselves and our posterity." In a Promethean spirit the people of Megalopolis are still building a "new order of the ages." This tradition has always included critical self-examination and a willingness to meet new challenges boldly.

If this tradition should fail us now, if complacency and resignation should set in, the great Megalopolitan experiment would be jeopardized. This would also jeopardize the hope that American ideals and know-how will lead the people of the world to a better, peaceful life.

If communities and individuals keep faith with this tradition, with the same endeavor and enthusiasm as in the past, they will build not only the largest and most prosperous but also the most livable and brightest city region ever to inspire the world.

# Index Entries *in Italics* denote illustrations

Printed in the United States of America. Press of Judd & Detweiler, Inc., Washington, D.C.

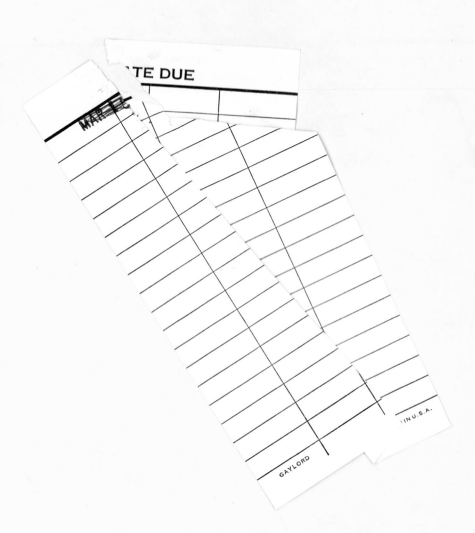

DATE DUE

GAYLORD

IN U.S.A.